A GUIDE TO BUDGETING

Get Out of Debt

and Live Your

Best Life on

What You Earn

BY

Jonathan M. Tinsley

Copyright © by Jonathan M. Tinsley 2024. All rights reserved.

TABLE OF CONTENTS

Introduction

Our finances affect every part of our lives. Everything we do, including attending classes and covering our housing, food, and clothing expenses, is funded by the money we make. We all know how important money is to people. Positivity about the financial world and sound money management are traits that will help you in any circumstance. Whether we like it or not, our degree of financial independence influences a lot of the decisions we make in life. At a certain point in your life, you may have heard or spoken something to the effect that money isn't essential.

While this seems like a great concept in theory, money is necessary for a variety of reasons. I'd like to tell you a little story that revolves around the importance of money.

Emily was a tiny child who lived in Beaufort, a charming but isolated city. Emily has been looking for it for almost twenty years, but she still hasn't located it. At fifteen, she began to sweat to provide for her family. To help her mom out a little bit, she decided to teach kindergarten after school. Emily's life is always a precarious balance between her ideal and real selves. Her imagination is constantly creating stories, such as fairy tales and what-ifs, more than what her mouth can say.

 In actuality, though, she is engrossed in a variety of physically demanding occupations.

Emily was in the sixth standard and needed to learn how to cook because her mom owned a tailoring shop. If her mother missed the deadlines, she also brought the appropriate customer's home with stitched clothes. She worked for three years as a milkmaid. She used to get up at four in the morning and return home by seven. She has been covering her rent, utilities, water, health care, and network costs for nearly twenty years. She has been managing the family's monthly spending. It just takes a few extraordinary, out-of-the-ordinary medical emergencies, family disputes, or religious customs to cause a financial dent that takes years to repair. She even does all of this without complaining. She eventually lost faith in all religions, customs, and relatives. Life teaches her that nothing will be free until she works hard. Her life was not miraculously changed by a ceremony or a relative. Even still, Emily never loses up on her dreams despite her depressing days spent pursuing wealth. Money determines her friends, her schooling, and the people she spends time with. She is friends with very few people. Even though she gives each person her whole attention and speaks to them with great care, she rarely takes anyone with her outside of time and space. She thinks that her sole safety and sanity are humility and honesty. She therefore never lies or tries to influence events to her advantage, no matter what the circumstance. Although the experience taught her a great deal, she still chooses to be humble and truthful with both herself and other people.

Sadly, Emily's decisions about her work are similarly driven by money rather than her excitement. Despite having a natural aptitude for teaching, she was unable to pursue her dream of teaching since she put her family's needs first. Dreams are far too expensive for the average person to afford in a place like America. She made a mistake by entering the chaotic business world, but she hasn't accomplished anything significant there either. If she hadn't succumbed to her romantic instincts, she could have accomplished more in the industry. She foolishly spent her money and salary for the last five years on a fantasy. On the other hand, she had to start from zero to grow. She did strengthen herself and completed a lot of stuff. She was unable to stockpile anything for the wet days, though. However, she ignored all of her goals and joys in favor of pursuing money. She enjoys reading books about classic literature. She enjoys flipping through a few pages in her small collection of her best novels.

Individuals are individuals; they always have something wrong to complain about and demand more from everyone and everything. She sometimes thinks that her mother at least accepts her for who she is. It is somewhat of a revelation to her as, although her parents raised her with varying degrees of awareness and sensibilities, they eventually cannot relate to so many of the things she does and force their failures upon her. She never had a nice response when someone asked her what she wanted. She truly takes care of her needs without asking for their help because she has been working and earning money for her parents. However, she prioritizes them before herself, thus all she wants is for her loved ones; she is unable to articulate what she actually, her true desires are not enormous wealth, a home, a car, or even a family; rather, she aspires to be a beacon of hope for many people by inspiring and encouraging others to follow their dreams and have faith in humanity. Had it not been for her parents' senseless arrogance amid her town, society, and family, she would have gone away from it all and volunteered to help people. The people in whom she put her trust or who she selflessly loved consistently betray her. Her parents depend on her for their comfort and are always complaining that she isn't capable of managing the household or starting a family of her own. She made every effort to demonstrate that, in the end, nothing counts until one reaches a socially respectable living standard. She can't bring herself to act against her instincts and feelings, not even after falling so many times. If she had relied on the relationships of a few important people to further her career, it would have been her greatest failure. She would have been in a significantly superior cultural grade. But she never could have used people's time or trust for her gain because of what she had learned all along. She often questions whether enduring all of this suffering is worthwhile in achieving her ultimate goal of dying. She is perfectly aware that it isn't! She occasionally longs to be free of her bulky meat costume. She looks forward to the day when she is not asked to provide for anyone's financial needs.

The harshest critics Emily has ever had in her life are her parents, who constantly call her an enormous failure. She is sick and tired of having people put increasing pressure on her instead of encouraging her to do what she loves. She is interested in everything after a while save for Disney cartoon characters and the Middle Earth created by Tolkien. Because Disney characters feel real and enduring, and because Middle-earth appears truer. She detests remaining friends with those who criticize her.

She is acutely aware of her shortcomings and the world around her. She doesn't need anyone's help to understand why or what went wrong. She has made a lot of mistakes, yet she is unable to give up on the causes she is passionate about. She finds meaning in the small things she spends money on, which give her great joy and a reason to get out of bed every day, in addition to her pointless daily routine of taking care of her family's financial needs. In the end, the world just cares about how much money she is worth—what she is made of is irrelevant!

I recognize that each of us has goals and desires in life, but some of us are limited by the numerous expenses we must pay to survive. Money affects all aspects of our lives, and the more adept we are at managing it, the better. While some of us are burdened by our demanding careers, others by family and relational issues and all that goes along with it, the key lesson to take away from this is that money counts in all of them. While it's true that some of us may never become millionaires or billionaires, everyone can achieve financial independence and have the comfortable, happy lives they truly desire. Gaining knowledge about money, its functions, and how to use it for your advantage is the first step towards achieving this.

This book focuses on budgeting, which is a cost-and income-based spending plan. Some say it's a projection of how much you will earn and spend over a specific period. You must acknowledge that the most important tool you have for building wealth or achieving financial freedom is your income. I will explain to you in the next chase peers how budgeting can help you achieve financial freedom.

Chapter 1

A Different Perspective

First and foremost, before we can begin to develop a new perspective or picture of our money or earnings, we must first grasp what they are and how they work. Money. What is it? Dirty paper: a tool to attain goals; a precious commodity; a mechanism to keep score; an opportunity... There are a lot of diverse perceptions about money. My favorite definition is that money is merely an idea supported by trust. Where there is no confidence, money has no worth. Money is fundamentally what people think it is. How we regard money impacts how we deal with it, and how we interact with it will decide whether we have it or not. Money is how we store energy; we have put it to work when the recipient does not have a reasonable object to trade of value. It all started with bargaining I gave the doctor 3 hens to make my daughter healthier. If everyone did this imagine the puppy "mess". So, he now asks for a product that everyone agrees to accept we call that money (even if gold or anything else is utilized) If the doctor is particularly good and fast, he now collects tons of easily exchangeable money rather than chickens. Now when he needs a service or commodity rather than trying to offload hens, he arranges how much money and exchanges that for what he wants. That recipient can now utilize it in a transaction for what they need, and the money passes around...So the more rounded one has, simply implies they have worked, long, hard, smart, or all the above and created excess; they can now utilize in trade for more of the products they desire. Paper money only has value because all of humanity has determined that it has value. Inherently, there's no value in paper money. You can't consume paper money. You can't clothe yourself with paper money (although, I guess if you acquired enough of it, you could wrap yourself up in it like toilet paper…). You can't create a house out of paper. Money is not significant to dogs agricultural animals, or germs. Nonetheless, money is one of the major factors that keep the world in order. Rich individuals who've never been poor don't comprehend why impoverished people stay poor. They recognize people may have suffered, but they generally don't comprehend why you would let that pain continue decade after decade. Surely poverty should push you to succeed. They don't know what debt feels like in your actual name, as opposed to an LLC. They don't realize the weight of dread every time a letter drops through the door. They don't know how worrying about money zaps you of liturgy and self-esteem. The flip sides to this is what impoverished people don't comprehend about the rich. It isn't just MONEY that separates individuals. That's how they look at life. Their attitudes and views about the navigate skills and possibilities. About people and the world and how to best navigate it.

There was this family who was all rich and enjoyed a luxurious life. The father was brilliant and hardworking, and the mother worked with him. They got some pocket money, just like every other parent, and it was a good amount. The parents were extremely opulent and were high-level luxurious spendthrifts also. They were earning big and thus they were giving their kids a lot to enjoy. Their pocket money was just so high that they could exist without studying and doing the job. These kids were smart too like their parents.

There was something unusual in the youngsters though. They were individuals who had studied alongside a diverse range of classmates, and they were friends with almost all of them. The parents worked hard but fate had another idea. The company was bankrupt overnight with all their money invested fully turning into nothing more than a few hundred dollars.

They had liabilities and loans piling up on their heads with nowhere to look. Everything inside their house had been taken, leaving only them house. The youngsters were smart as indicated previously and they recognized that the money they received was far more than required. Both the youngsters had saved the money fearing such a time. What was the money amounting to? It was similar to their parent's 6-month profits. Their parents were shocked by the money left. But this time the youngsters requested their parents to start again with their friends' parents. They sold the house and satisfactorily lived their life paying off the liabilities. Soon thanks to their educated parents and their spouses they came back to a much better stage in life financially. But this time their parents had learned from their kids the art and value of saving money. They maintained the pocket money identical for the youngsters but lowered their spending substantially. It was a typical case of learning from children and the parents were thrilled to know that their children already knew this element of life.

I want you to understand that money comes with a lot of negative implications, but you get to choose how you interpret your earnings. If you feel terrible about your wages, you can make a change just like the kid's parents did.

Understanding your money mindset

Our perspective can substantially affect the way we handle our finances. Your money mindset refers to the attitudes, ideas, and emotions that drive your financial habits and behaviors and is shaped by your upbringing, personal experiences, cultural background, and overall attitude toward money. But, despite our money management being so impacted by our money mindset, many of us might not take the time to explore our thoughts and beliefs around our finances to determine our money mindset.

Understanding your thinking around money and debt is a vital step to financial management. Unmanageable debt, for example, isn't merely a financial issue; it may be occasionally tied to your money perspective. For example, some people take up debt to cope with mental concerns such as worry, anxiety, or low self-esteem which can lead to a cycle of expenditure and debt. This behavior can be tough to break.

Others may take up debt as a strategy to cope with unanticipated financial difficulties or to maintain a specific quality of living. This might be especially true for those who feel pressure to keep up with their peers or maintain a specific image. These practices can lead to a reliance on debt and an inability to live within one's means.

Debt can also be a result of insufficient financial literacy and a lack of resources to obtain skills in money management. Without the knowledge of how to build up an efficient budget and plan for your future finances, it can be easy to go into debt without recognizing the implications.

Understanding your money perspective is key to overcoming the cycle of overspending and excessive debt. By addressing the underlying emotional difficulties that drive our spending habits, we can begin to establish healthy coping mechanisms and financial habits.

The diverse money mindsets

Your money mindset is affected by your upbringing, personal experiences, cultural background, and overall attitude toward money. Here are several prevalent money mindsets:

The Saver: The saver attitude is defined by a willingness to save money and plan for the future. Those with this perspective tend to be more cautious with their spending and are generally focused on building up their money. In other circumstances, individuals may feel concerned about spending money and tend to avoid spontaneous purchases. While saving is a good financial habit, excessive saving can also lead to lost opportunities or even a fear of spending money when it is necessary.

The Spender: The spender mindset is characterized by a want to spend money on experiences or items. People who think like this usually enjoy shopping and might find it difficult to resist making impulsive buys. They may feel a sense of exhilaration or pleasure while spending money, which can lead to overspending and insurmountable debt.

The Indifferent: The indifferent mindset is defined by a lack of interest or worry about money. Those with this mindset may not worry much about their financial condition and may be less likely to track their spending or savings. They may be pleased with their existing financial condition, even if it means living paycheck to paycheck.

The Borrower: The borrower mindset is characterized by a predisposition to rely on credit and loans to finance their lifestyle. Those with this perspective may be comfortable with taking on debt and might not be excessively concerned about paying it back. They may also have a hard time discerning between wants and needs, which can lead to overspending and excessive debt.

It's crucial to keep in mind that there are several money mindsets that people may display based on their circumstances or stage of life. Numerous other categories of money mindset exist, such as the five money personalities. The most crucial thing is to take the time to comprehend your money mindset to assist you find places where you can make changes to improve your financial mindset, regardless of the sorts of money mindset and personalities you encounter.

Scarcity and Abundance theory is another popular lens through which to view money thinking. The scarcity mindset is centered on scarcity and the anxiety that comes with running out of something, which can cause hoarding or excessive purchasing habits. Conversely, the abundant mindset emphasizes thankfulness and the idea that there is enough for everyone, which may result in a more carefree attitude toward your money.

The worry of running out of resources, particularly money, is the hallmark of the scarcity mindset. This worry may cause one to engage in bad habits like hoarding or excessive spending. People who have a scarcity mindset could believe that they can't enjoy what they have because they need to continually have more money. They might also struggle to save money and be prone to impulsive purchases. On the other hand, when applied sparingly, a scarcity mindset might encourage people to become more economical with their expenditures.

A mindset of abundance is defined by the conviction that there is always sufficient for everyone. A more carefree attitude toward money may result from this way of thinking. Individuals who possess an abundant mindset may also exhibit greater generosity and a willingness to distribute their assets to others. An abundance mentality, nevertheless, can also result in excessive spending and unwise financial risk-taking.

In conclusion, your financial habits can be greatly influenced by your mindset—whether it is one of scarcity or abundance. Even though each mindset has advantages and disadvantages, it's critical to identify the mindset with which you identify and strive to challenge the more negative financial behaviors while fostering more favorable ones.

A better relationship with money and financial situation management depends on your ability to recognize and understand your money attitude. Consider your relationship with money first. What attitudes and ideas do you have regarding money? What are your thoughts on borrowing, spending, and saving? You can obtain an understanding of the attitudes and ideas that influence your financial choices by thinking back on your relationship with money. This might assist you in determining any harmful habits or viewpoints that might be affecting your financial security.

If you discover, for instance, that you tend to overspend, you might look into any habits or beliefs you may have regarding emotional or rapid fulfillment. On the other hand, if you find yourself saving frequently, you might want to investigate if your saving behaviors are motivated by a need for financial stability or a fear of shortage. After determining your financial mindset, you may begin to confront any negative attitudes or habits that might be preventing you from reaching your full potential.

This could entail creating a budget or financial plan, altering your spending patterns, or seeing a specialist.

In the end, developing an awareness of your financial mindset is a continuous process that calls for introspection as well as a readiness to change and advance. However, by taking the time to consider how you feel about money, you may learn a lot about how you behave financially and make adjustments that will help you in the long run.

Your financial thinking is a major factor in how you relate to debt. Gaining insight into your financial attitude and controlling negative thoughts and actions will help you create better financial habits and make the initial moves toward debt relief.

Money-related misconceptions

Money has been the focus of many myths and misconceptions for generations, which has led to many individuals developing negative attitudes toward wealth and money management. This is true even within the Muslim community, as people with varying backgrounds, occupations, and social strata have different attitudes on money that are frequently influenced by their own experiences.

There is an Islamic perspective on money and how it should be acquired and used, regardless of personal preferences. Some widespread misunderstandings about money are situated in the midst of these.

1. The source of all evil is money

"Money is the root of all evil" is a proverb that has been handed down through the ages.

Many think that having money forces you to do unthinkable things.

People who hold this perspective do not seize opportunities to earn money because they believe individuals who do so are avaricious. Their notion that the pieces of paper they are holding are evil makes them desire to get rid of money quickly (maybe by spending and donating).

Furthermore, Muslims who hold this perspective regard rich Muslims as individuals who just care about this life rather than the afterlife. They think that having money will keep them from worshiping Allah.

Reality: Not all evil stems from a want of money. The sentence itself misinterprets 1 Timothy 6:10, a scriptural passage. Rather than money being the source of all evil, it states that "the love of money is the root of all evil." The proper passage provides a rather clear explanation. Money cannot turn you away from worshiping Allah or cause you to sin. It is merely a slip of paper. It matters how you handle money and how you relate to it. Loving money is, in fact, the source of all evil.

Many affluent individuals are dedicated to uplifting others out of poverty, supporting charitable causes, and lending a hand to others. You will probably discover that some of these rich Muslims use their income to give Zakat and Sadaqat, construct mosques, support individuals to perform the Hajj and

Umrah, and fortify family bonds. They are drawing nearer to Allah via all of these deeds, not away from Him.

2. There's lots of time for you to save

Another common misperception held by some young, diligent people is that saving money is superfluous, especially if they don't intend to retire very soon. As a result, they don't think saving is important.

Reality: Starting to save right now is the best advice anyone could give. Don't put off saving money, whether it's for a future project or trip, retirement, or something else entirely. Financially, you will do better the earlier you start.

Remember that time is of the essence, thus it is imperative that you start saving as soon as possible, regardless of how much money you make. The lure of a more opulent lifestyle grows as your income rises. No matter how little you save, it all adds up to improve your financial situation.

3. Happier people have more money

Affluence is frequently linked to happiness. While some people are happy with just having enough money to cover their expenses, others think that having more money will make you happier. They believe that living in a house, driving a nice automobile, and leading an opulent lifestyle inevitably translates into contentment.

Truth: Everyone desires wealth, but having an unhealthy love for money can lead to unhappiness. Believing that having more money will make you happier will only lead to an unending cycle of unmet wants. In the end, you will fall into a void of melancholy and emptiness.

4. Before you can begin investing, you need a sizable amount of money.

One of the common misconceptions about money is that those who are in more need shouldn't think about investing. Having insufficient funds shouldn't ever stop you from making investments. The basic goal of investing is long-term returns, and the truth is that you don't need much to get started. Fractional shares are an investment option that lets you purchase parts of shares and gradually increase your position.

Setting away a certain portion of your income for investments is a smart idea, even if it's just $1, and you should gradually develop the investing habit. Recall that no investment is too tiny.

5. You have to be in your 60s to retire.

Some people think that you can truly start to slow down and enjoy life only after you become 65, at which point you can retire. Although it varies by area, retirement often knocks on your door at age 65. For instance, the retirement age in the US and the UK is between 62 and 67, but there is no restriction on retiring early. It matters what you do to ensure an early retirement for yourself.

6. You lack the necessary qualities to be affluent.

Another myth is that some people believe they are incapable of becoming wealthy because they do not possess the necessary abilities. But when you ask them what skills they don't have, they will give you an explanation. In reality, though, what you'll discover is that they lack the motivation to put their skills to use. This way of thinking is unhealthy.

Reality: There are no shortcuts to wealth; those who aspire to achieve it must be willing to work hard. Consider this: • What could go wrong if I choose to accept the risk of putting in long hours of work every day?

• What will happen most favorably if my efforts are successful?

• I can choose to stand out, so why am I making such an effort to blend in like everyone else?

• What are my innate abilities, and how can I use them to my advantage?

Rich people typically have a can-do attitude and prefer an abundance mindset over a scarcity mindset, while poor people frequently display a negative outlook and write themselves off.

7. Security = Money

Many times, people mistake having money for security. They contend that material wealth elevates a person above all hardships. Is this possible to be true?

Reality: Being wealthy does not equate to security. You might still be unwell and confined to bed. Never will you have enough cash to be in charge of everything. Rich people frequently pass away from fatal illnesses; nothing is truly secure. As Muslims, we are aware that Allah is supreme and that He can test anybody He pleases.

Yes, having riches makes you more comfortable than the average person, but it does not make you invincible.

8. Your worries decrease as you accumulate wealth

Many people think that when you have more money, you should worry less. For example, some believe money can overcome any obstacle and solve all issues. This is a serious misconception, to be sure.

Reality: The truth begs to differ. More money usually equates to more concerns. The biggest concern of all for a Muslim is being held accountable. It is important to think about the fact that on the day of judgment, one will be held accountable for every dollar spent in this life.

9. Debt is commonplace.

Some people think that taking out loans and having credit card debt is normal and shouldn't be concerning.

Reality: Since it can ruin your finances, this misunderstanding is arguably the worst. Making it a habit to purchase something you cannot afford is a surefire path to financial disaster. Experian estimates that in 2022, customers' total debt will have increased by more than $1 trillion, a remarkable rise not witnessed in more than ten years.

Avoid the temptation to normalize high debt levels since this will keep you from accumulating wealth and will need you to devote the majority of your resources to debt settlement. It's also very important to stay within your means.

10. You put in a lot of work and should be able to afford lovely things.

Those who put in a lot of labor often reward themselves with "nice things." When we talk about good things in this sense, we mean pricey things for someone who wants to accumulate riches. However, the thing itself is of little value to them because their priorities are self-fulfillment and social validation.

The truth is that some people who use their hard-earned money to purchase "nice things" for themselves barely make ends meet.

Rich people are renowned for leading thrifty lives; Warren Buffett, Carlos Slim, and Mark Zuckerberg are just a few examples. Gifts are a wonderful way to treat oneself, but in the long run, learning to postpone gratification can yield the greatest rewards.

Understanding the true nature of money can have a huge impact on our financial decisions and overall well-being. One essential aspect of our lives is money. Never forget that using money wisely according to Islamic principles can lead to a wealth of chances and blessings. However, an overwhelming love of money and worldly belongings can be harmful to a person's mental and spiritual health.

I used to be skeptical about the benefits of having an abundant money mindset. I still recall asking myself, "How in the world can changing a few ideas and beliefs result in getting more money?"

I believed that asking for a raise from my employer, getting a second job, or winning the lottery were the only things that could truly improve my financial circumstances.

I didn't believe in this money-belief nonsense, whatever it was.

However, my interest took off when I decided to become an entrepreneur and began to understand the value and influence of money tales and an abundance mindset.

As an entrepreneur in particular, I've found that success stories can either help you expand and generate more revenue or hinder you from doing so.

I started to realize the financial myths that I had been taught and told as a child, which essentially said that money was something that should be kept rather than squandered.

My father, an accountant, has always advised me to put up as much money as I can for my future, including for a house or car, a child, and retirement.

For this reason, when I became older, I realized that I didn't like to spend money.

I was under a lot of stress having to make all these decisions.

Is this something I need? Is the cost justified? Can't locate a better offer somewhere else? Is now the right time to purchase it? Do I merit this?

Hence, if I didn't need anything, I would usually choose the cheapest choice and feel terrible about it.

The majority of the time, though, I wasn't particularly happy with the item I decided to purchase because it was either awful or simply wasn't my top choice.

The hilarious thing was that I didn't save any money because, in most cases, the item I had purchased didn't last more than a few months, meaning I had to repeat the entire cycle of worry, shame, and paralysis by analysis.

The only item I overspent on was makeup; I could easily afford a ninety-dollar eye shadow palette, but forty dollars for sneakers was just too much.

I became aware that I needed to alter my money stories and live more abundantly to attract greater financial prosperity, freedom, and joy when I began reading about money stories, the law of attraction, and an abundance vs. scarcity attitude.

The sheer joy this exquisitely colored pallet of eyeshadows

brought me was indescribable. And for years, I used it every day.

Therefore, for me, developing an abundant attitude also meant extending this mentality of a makeup palette to other aspects of my life.

The Mentality of Finance

Our financial decisions can be greatly influenced by our attitudes regarding money, which are intricately linked to our emotions. Numerous elements, including our upbringing, cultural influences, and individual experiences, influence these attitudes. People who view money as a source of security, for example, might be more likely to place a high value on saving and prudent investing techniques. However, people who see money as a status or power symbol may be more likely to take chances or buy ostentatious items.

Fear, greed, anxiety, guilt, and other negative emotions can have a big influence on our financial decisions. Our inability to take calculated risks due to fear may limit our ability to expand and make investments. Greed can cause impulsive decision-making, putting short-term gains ahead of financial stability. Excessive spending can be a coping method for anxiety, and shame can cause us to make financial decisions based more on social pressure than on good judgment.

Making sensible financial decisions requires an understanding of and ability to control these emotions. One can make more logical decisions that are in line with their long-term financial objectives by developing emotional awareness and identifying emotional triggers.

Making wise financial decisions requires us to control our emotions when it comes to money. Emotions frequently impair our judgment and cause us to act impulsively, which may not be in line with our long-term financial objectives. We can make more deliberate and logical financial judgments if we are aware of our emotions and have techniques to control them.

A significant aspect of the human experience is emotion. Some of the greatest cultural and scientific achievements of humanity have been impacted by them. However, if they are not handled properly, they can also have a detrimental effect during uncertain and stressful situations.

Thousands of historical examples show how emotions have shaped both the finest and worst of American situations. For example, Francis Scott Key, inspired by witnessing the American flag flying high during a furious battle with the British, composed "The Star-Spangled Banner". The leaders of the American civil rights, women's rights, and LGBTQ rights movements were driven forward in their endeavors by a plethora of emotions, including anger and resentment. But increased violence against Muslims and Asians was also a result of the COVID-19 outbreak and the 9/11 tragedy's heightened concerns and anxieties.

Imagine the impact emotions can have on your daily life, including your finances, if they can alter history and bring out people's worst parts. You'll be in a better position to make emotionally sound financial decisions if you examine how emotions affect your thoughts and behavior.

Recognize That Your Emotions Can Impact Your Decisions

A 2007 Journal management study revealed that the ability to recognize one's own emotions contributed to one's ability to regulate one's own biases, which in turn led to better decision-making.

Wechter refers to this process as "making conscious the unconscious"; it involves facing your feelings and ideas head-on so you can see how they affect you.

"Emotions are neither good nor bad," she clarified. "Knowing the feelings that influence your decisions is more important than trying to remain emotionless. To view things as realistically as possible, be clear about the source of your sentiments."

However, feelings pass, but the consequences of your financial choices may last a lifetime or be hard to reverse. This is why it's so important to be conscious of and regulate your emotions when making these decisions.

Focus on the facts rather than your feelings.

Many times, all it takes to break the grip your emotions have on your actions is to focus just on the facts.

Sometimes all it takes to demonstrate the logic of your financial plan is to dissect the figures. Chun frequently assists clients who are apprehensive about using tax-advantaged wealth transfer options because they believe they may use the funds in the future.

"I try to get clients to objectively understand how they are, not how they feel they are," he said. "If I can demonstrate to them that they have more than enough money to meet their needs for the rest of their lives, it creates a chance to take other sensible actions related to wealth transfer, risk management, and charitable planning. It removes emotional obstacles."

Chun advises paying attention to the facts at hand if you believe that your emotions are interfering with your ability to think clearly about an issue. You can evaluate the circumstance more clearly and maintain these specifics in mind by putting all you know to be true in writing. Alternatively, you could discuss matters with a trusted friend or relative to get a different viewpoint.

Recognize Your Financial Scripts

Your parents, other family members, significant life events, and society as a whole probably taught you valuable lessons about money and wealth when you were growing up, shaping your fundamental beliefs about money. Certain financial psychologists call these teachings "money scripts."

In certain situations, is almost impossible to disentangle feelings from facts, no matter how hard you try. It's critical to identify your emotional triggers if you believe that they are impairing your judgment.

Your financial life doesn't have to be dictated by your feelings. Your behavior is driven by money scripts, which you can understand and use to replace negative thinking and bad behaviors with positive ones.

So where do you even start? Start by asking yourself questions and honestly responding to them in a journal or on paper to start an internal money dialogue.

To assist you in getting started, consider these questions: • What is the function that money plays in your life and how do you use it now?

• When did you first remember learning about money?

• What financial lessons did your parents teach you? additional family members?

• How did you feel about your upbringing and what was your financial status?

• What financial fear do you have the most?

• Why do particular feelings or actions surface when money is involved?

• What fundamental principles do you uphold? Do your financial practices align with those principles?

Awareness is the first step toward change. You can start to retrain your behaviors or replace them completely once you comprehend their underlying causes.

Understand Your Relationship with Money to Gain Self-Awareness

Wealth planning is based on data and statistics, but it's also critical to consider your attitudes and convictions around money. Since almost everything that people do involves money in one way or another and since people are inherently emotional beings, money is a very personal matter for them. People spend a great deal of their life pursuing it.

Working with a financial advisor who can discourage you from making poor, emotional decisions is crucial as your wealth increases. Furthermore, further therapy with a therapist who specializes in financial concerns may help you comprehend the underlying causes of specific behaviors. The way we handle money is similar to the way we handle power, love, and other relationships. How we use money says a lot about us, so it's worth understanding.

Modifying viewpoints

Having a growth mentality can help you become more financially successful and improve your overall financial situation.

Even though money is a big part of our everyday lives, making financial decisions like paying off debt, using credit cards sensibly, or purchasing a home can become complicated. As a result, people frequently make financial mistakes that could have a detrimental impact on their financial security. Here's when having a growth mentality is useful.

A growth mindset is essentially the conviction that, with commitment and hard work, your abilities and skills can be enhanced. Individuals who have a growth mindset are willing to take chances and explore new possibilities to achieve their goals because they view failure as a chance for learning and development. A fixed mindset, on the other hand, is the conviction that your talents and abilities are intrinsic and unchangeable, which might cause you to be afraid of failing and reluctant to take chances.

Generally speaking, a growth mindset individual will:

• A person with a growth mentality will view failure as an opportunity to improve rather than respond negatively to criticism or failure.

• A growth mindset acknowledges that one's abilities are not fixed and drives oneself to always learn new things.

• Rather than viewing another person's achievement as a threat or cause for jealousy, someone with a development mindset views it as an inspiration.

Success in the financial world is not solely dependent on income; it also depends on your mindset and behavior. You can overcome financial obstacles, gain knowledge from experiences, and accomplish your financial objectives by cultivating a growth mentality. Here's how to succeed financially and cultivate a growth attitude.

What connection exists between financial well-being and a growth mindset?

You start to think differently about how you talk to yourself and other people about financial success when you start examining the distinctions between a growth mindset and a fixed mindset. Think about this: you will be less able to save and invest your money if your entire

attention is on paying off debt. Consequently, having a growth mindset alters your perspective on money and fosters productivity and motivation.

Financial well-being and a growth mindset are closely associated since the former promotes the acquisition of the knowledge and attitudes required for successful financial management. Individuals who have a growth mindset think that they can become better at something by working hard, being persistent, and picking up lessons from mistakes. They are inspired to take on new tasks, look for educational possibilities, and endure in the face of failures by this mindset. In terms of financial well-being, a growth mindset can assist people in acquiring the abilities and habits required for achievement.

• In the upcoming chapters, I'll be sharing several secrets with you that require a willingness to take calculated risks to reach financial goals.

• You must stop seeing errors and setbacks as indicators of ineptitude and instead see them as chances to improve.

• You must be receptive to fresh perspectives and chances that can assist them in bettering their financial circumstances, like picking up new expertise or connecting with other industry experts.

• You must possess resilience to bounce back from financial failures and carry on working toward your objectives.

All things considered, a growth mindset can assist people in acquiring the knowledge and practices required for financial success, which can ultimately result in greater financial security and well-being.

Ultimately, a growth attitude maintains healthy financial and interpersonal relationships. A growth mentality encourages taking constructive action rather than dwelling on one's shortcomings, particularly about others. A growth mentality will assist you in creating attainable goals and creating positive momentum, as opposed to concentrating on your lack of money or feeling overburdened while avoiding debt.

How can you adopt a development mentality to enhance your financial health?

Developing a learning attitude is the first step toward bettering your financial situation. This is admitting that while you might not know everything, you can still grow your financial knowledge and abilities over time by learning from others. Reading books, going to seminars,

or enrolling in online courses on personal finance are some ways to get started. A financial advisor can help you comprehend your options and create a personalized financial strategy, so you should consult with one.

You need to form sound financial habits, such as saving money, staying out of debt, and keeping to a budget, to retain financial discipline. You can accomplish your long-term financial objectives by doing this. Establishing automated savings plans to deposit money into your savings account every month is one method of putting financial discipline into reality. Additionally, you can cut back on wasteful spending by not going out to eat or buying clothes you don't need.

When you have a growth mindset, you are constantly looking for new ways to save money or boost your revenue. This could be launching a side business, making real estate or stock investments, or figuring out how to cut costs. To increase your income, you may, for instance, look into doing freelance work in your leisure time or look into methods to reduce the amount you pay each month for your bills.

It's typical to encounter obstacles or failures when it comes to money and resources. However, you may use

these difficulties as teaching opportunities if you embrace a growth attitude. When things don't go as planned, don't give up; instead, give it some thought, analyze what went wrong, and figure out how to approach it better the next time. You'll become more adept at making financial decisions and more robust to obstacles in your financial life as a result of this.

To reach your financial objectives, you concentrate on and hone your abilities when you have a growth mentality. If you are skilled in marketing, for instance, you can utilize it to advertise your company or side project. You can find ways to boost your income and create a career around something you enjoy by highlighting your abilities.

Having conversations and establishing connections with people who have similar financial objectives to yours can yield a wealth of information and guidance. To meet like-minded people, go to financial seminars, sign up for clubs or online forums, or join groups. You may stay motivated, pick-up new ideas and insights, and learn from the experiences of others by maintaining these ties.

You may maintain your motivation by setting up a system of rewards for yourself when you reach a financial milestone. No matter how tiny, acknowledge and celebrate your accomplishments, and keep in mind how far you have come. Additionally, you can picture your future financial prosperity and the advantages it will bring to your life. This might support you in maintaining your enthusiasm and commitment to your objectives in the face of difficulties.

You are prepared to modify your financial strategy as necessary to reach your objectives if you have a growth mentality. This entails remaining adaptable and receptive to new opportunities, even if they weren't initially planned for. For instance, you might need to adjust your financial objectives or look for other sources of income if you lose your employment. You can overcome unforeseen setbacks and keep working toward your goals if you can remain flexible.

Your financial well-being can be significantly impacted by cultivating a development mentality. To keep a positive outlook, keep in mind to concentrate on your abilities, seek out chances to learn and develop, interact with others, and cultivate thankfulness.

It might be difficult to have a positive outlook on money and wealth-building. It's crucial to keep in mind that our attitudes and views about money are frequently

influenced by our upbringing and prior experiences and that changing them might take time and effort. Observe the plenty in everything in life, not just financial wealth. Numerous factors, such as love, community, environment, and joy, contribute to abundance. Recalling something as basic as "I am a success because I am breathing!"

could help you concentrate on what really matters.

We will explore a realistic strategy for managing your income in the upcoming chapter, so you can use it to achieve your goals. After discussing the mentality adjustment, let's go on to the following phase and provide our earnings role-specific purposes. Let's talk about a potent budgeting idea. Consider your earnings as members of a team, each with a distinct role to complete as you progress financially.

Chapter 2

Get Your Pennies to Work

We talked about how our thinking may impact all aspects of our lives, not just our finances, in the first chapter. Living "paycheck to paycheck" may indicate that you have developed a scarcity mentality around finances. You may have gone through an experience in the past that has shaped the way you think about money today. You now function from that mental place as a result, which gives you less-than-ideal outcomes.

You can discover that you are reluctant to spend money or that you spend the majority of it as soon as it enters your checking account. Although there are undoubtedly emotional aspects to this, your perspective on how you earn and spend money is the most crucial factor of all.

You will constantly be focused on the idea that you will never have enough if you have a scarcity mindset. A lot of people are unaware of this, yet everyone has a relationship with money! If you treat it badly, it will vanish from you. Good care will make it flourish, support you through difficult times, and more! Individuals differ in how they relate to money. Some people are born savers, having extra cash at the end of the month. With one more month to go before the money runs out, some people are spenders. If you haven't already, keep a thirty-day journal of your expenditures to identify your spending habits. Keep track of your daily expenses and purchases in a diary, log, or phone note. Keeping a record of your spending will support your next move. The secret is to make every dollar you make work, which is impossible to achieve without a thorough understanding of budgeting.

One essential component of managing personal finances is

budgeting. This financial plan assists individuals and families in allocating their earnings to debt repayment, savings, and expenses. We take some time in this post to recognize the value of budgeting as a tool that helps you manage your finances, stay focused on your financial objectives, and act as a safety net for unforeseen costs. My goal is to provide you with the skills and information necessary for effective money management. This essay is intended for those who are new to budgeting or those who are looking to improve their current budget. We'll go over the fundamentals of budgeting, its significance, various budgeting techniques, how to make a good budget, and frequent budgeting obstacles. We'll also go over a few well-liked applications and tools for budgeting that help streamline and automate the process. The practice of planning how you will spend your money is called budgeting. Making sure you have enough money to meet your requirements and wants, entails striking a balance between your income and expenses. A budget is a roadmap that shows you how much you want to spend and how much you think you'll make over a given time frame, usually a month.

Budgeting plays a critical function in financial management. It acts as a financial roadmap, assisting you in allocating your money to several areas including savings, debt repayment, housing, food, and transportation. By assigning a purpose to each dollar, budgeting guarantees that you maximize your financial resources. Moreover, budgeting fosters financial literacy. It necessitates keeping track of your earnings and outlays, which can provide you with an accurate image of your financial status. This knowledge can assist you in making financially responsible decisions, such as determining where you need to allocate more money or where you can make savings. Budgeting is also a strategy for reaching financial objectives. A budget can assist you in achieving your financial objectives, whether they be emergency fund development, debt repayment, or vacation savings. You can see noticeable benefits and make consistent progress toward your goals by allocating a percentage of your monthly income to them.

Finally, creating a budget offers a safety net for unforeseen costs. There are many surprises in life, and not all of them are good. A medical cost, a car repair, or a job loss can completely destabilize your finances. However, you can put money aside for an emergency savings account with a budget, giving you a safety net in case of unforeseen circumstances.

One essential component of financial management is budgeting. In addition to helping, you reach your financial objectives and providing you control over your finances, it also fosters financial awareness and acts as a safety net for unforeseen costs.

One might ask. what makes budgeting crucial, then?

Controlling spending is one of the main advantages of budgeting. You can set aside particular percentages of your income for various expenses like groceries, entertainment, rent, and savings by making a budget. The amount that you can spend in each category without going above your salary is made evident by this allocation.

Additionally, budgeting promotes careful spending. It forces you to reconsider your purchases and determine whether they are necessary and within your price range. By practicing mindfulness, you can avoid making rash purchases and organize your expenditures according to your requirements and desires.

Budgeting also enables you to recognize and cut out wasteful spending. By tracking your spending, you may find that you're paying more than you anticipated on purchases. Recognizing these costs enables you to make subscription services, eating out, and other non-essential reductions and save money.

What part does budgeting play in reaching financial objectives?

A budget is essential to reaching financial objectives. A budget can assist you in achieving your objectives, whether they be creating an emergency fund, saving for a vacation, or preparing for a down payment on a home.

A portion of your money will always go toward your financial goals if you include them in your budget. With time, this regular saving can pile up and get you closer to your objectives.

You may keep track of your progress toward your objectives by using a budget. You may monitor your savings progress and the amount you still need to save, making any necessary adjustments to your budget to keep you on target. Budgeting can help reduce the overwhelming tension that comes with money. Having a clear understanding of your income and expenses might help you feel more in charge of your money.

Making a budget also guarantees that you have adequate cash on hand to pay your bills and other essential costs. The worry of living paycheck to paycheck and worrying about whether you'll be able to make ends meet can be removed with this certainty.

Budgeting also enables you to create an emergency fund, which serves as a safety net for unforeseen costs. Knowing that you have money set aside for unanticipated expenses like auto repairs, medical bills, or job loss can give you peace of mind.

Because it lowers financial stress, helps achieve financial goals, and controls expenditure, budgeting is crucial. By providing you with financial control, creating a budget can enhance your quality of life and financial stability.

One of my main financial habits that drives my entire life these days is budgeting. It wasn't always the case, though.

I had to suffer financial ruin before realizing the power of budgeting.

My family wasn't particularly wealthy, but we were a loving family nonetheless. Thus, I never received any financial education. I, at least, have no recollections of it. My mother may see it differently.

Furthermore, budgeting isn't a crucial early skill. You know you're doing okay when your only expenses are Donald Duck publications, Coke, and ice cream. Yes, it would have prevented me from becoming bankrupt in the future, but I didn't mind as a child.

I didn't bother learning about money management in school because I didn't have an allowance. And with whatever occasional cash presents I would get, I would buy meals, game CDs, computer parts, and internet cafes.

I worked a couple of jobs doing manual labor with some of my classmates later in high school, but nothing major, and I never really liked having a job. I was not one of those youngsters who were eager to leave home at a young age and become self-sufficient. My home life was fortunate, so I didn't see real money until after college.

After graduation, the prospect of working from home didn't seem all that intriguing. So, with a few hundred euros in my pocket and a huge bag filled with my belongings, I set off for Germany.

The idea was to settle permanently in Germany, and I even had several online anarchist pals in Leipzig that I could share housing with. I worked as a software engineer for approximately a month after moving into the backroom of an anarchist pub. The expenses were minimal and the income was good. Life was pleasant.

However, in reality, it wasn't, as at the time, I had no concept of what it meant to be an adult and support myself. I eventually had to leave Germany after less than a year because of circumstances that are best left for another time.

It was all a silly series of events, but at least I returned home with some cash in my bank account. I was able to relax and take it easy for the next several months. No employment, low expenses, no responsibilities, and no stress. I too didn't have a single life aim at the time, and I still think of this as maybe my happiest moment ever. Simple but happy.

Over the following few years, three things occurred: I began freelancing as a means of generating additional money; I subsequently launched a small business that had some success; and I received a modest amount of additional funding in exchange for helping with real estate from a cousin.

I didn't spend a lot on personal expenses, and since I operated my business alone at first, I didn't spend much on business expenses either. I didn't bother learning budgeting because the only two figures I saw were from my bank account statements, and they appeared to be fine. I was getting too comfortable. Can you afford to stick to your budget? Sort of. You can get by without a budget if your income is significantly more than your expenses. Though, would you wager on it continuing this way? You need to be on the lookout for things like losing your job, getting divorced, getting fired, your business failing, living over your means, crises, and large purchases.

In my situation, my bills came first. Over a few years, I grew complacent and increased my spending on both personal and business. I didn't purchase a yacht or anything major, but that's the issue.

It's simple to become disoriented by your spending when you're not monitoring your money. Furthermore, even modest expenses soon mount up. They combine.

In addition to taking up a few pricey hobbies, I began traveling. I started adding staff and taking on new projects, which led to a rise in my business expenses. Why wouldn't I, because I had the cash in my bank accounts?

Although it wasn't long-term viable, it wasn't an issue as long as the revenue continued to increase.

And it continued to expand.

After that, it ceased expanding.

Then it began to descend.

Not a single choice was the final factor. Seldom is it. Furthermore, it wasn't quite abrupt. It was a series of choices I made over a few years that caused it.

Initially, I became aware that I was unable to continue paying myself the amount I had been. Simply put, the company was no longer making enough money. Okay, not too good. However, I was certain that it was only a little slump, so I took no action.

Subsequently, the source of income diminished to the extent that I was forced to halt several current initiatives and terminate several contracts. Though I wasn't concerned about it, it was sad. I further reduced my pay and invested some of my own money in the company. I started working more than ever and cut my spending.

Nevertheless, nothing was improving. I started to worry that I wouldn't have enough money to pay my core team. I was correct, too. My finances ran out. Luckily, I could ask for assistance from a few pals. I increased my runway a little by taking out a couple of loans. Not yet desperate, though. I had a plan. It had to have been just a poor time.

Nevertheless, it wasn't.

Some of the following year was unpleasant. I tried a different approach after my first one failed. And still another. I was desperate now. I kept attempting everything, but nothing was successful.

I eventually had to begin terminating my key staff. To pay the salaries I owed, I ultimately had to take out a second loan from a friend. The least I could have done was that.

My business was over at this point. My romance ended at the same time. and a few additional items. I also collapsed because my identity was inextricably linked to my business.

I felt irreparably damaged, exhausted, indebted, and hopelessly miserable.

My worst identity issue to date occurred at that time.

The issue of keeping track of expenses

Let's talk about finances now; the tale of my recuperation is a narrative for another day.

From the beginning, I was aware that my lack of financial literacy contributed to my current situation.

Though not the primary one, it was a significant one. I lost money because I was irresponsible with it.

I pledged myself there and then: I will do everything in my power to ensure that my bad money management practices never lead me to ruin again.

I promised to learn how to create a budget.

Why not just track expenses using a budget?

Since I realized that keeping track of expenses is insufficient.

I kept a record of my spending for a few short periods. It never seemed to last though, and it was always a waste of time. I didn't have a purpose to track my expenses, therefore that was the reason.

My two issues in tracking expenses are as follows:

• There's hardly much benefit to checking your expenses when things are going well financially.

• Tracking your expenses won't help you if your finances are in disarray.

Allow me to clarify.

You don't have much of an incentive to keep track of your spending when you're not having financial difficulties.

It does tell you how much you spend on different items. It's also interesting to examine your expense breakdown, complete with charts if you're into data. However, it's not necessary for survival.

It's good to know you spent $350 on eating out last month, but that's just a figure. Is that a significant amount? Who knows, but when your bank account looks nice, who cares? (The way I was thinking led me into danger.)

However, the converse is also true:

Merely tracking your expenses won't help you when you're struggling to make ends meet. Keep track of anything you want, but when you're seeing $3.50 in your bank account a week before the next paycheck, it doesn't help to know that you overspent on takeout last week.

You may feel guilty about it for a while, but it won't stop you from doing it in the future. Simply put, the feedback loop is too long. Examining the data after the event does not assist you in resolving the fundamental issues with your expenditure.

NB! Not that keeping track of expenses is pointless. Even so, it increases your financial awareness. If you follow through on it long enough, you'll begin to notice trends that might influence you to alter your behavior. But for now, it's of no use.

I never really got into spending tracking because of this. Either I wasn't broken and watching my costs wouldn't have mattered, or I was doing well enough financially that I didn't care about the specific figures.

I needed an upgrade from spending tracking.

The solution was to create a budget.

Making a budget is the way

Budgeting is whatever the opposite of post-factum spending tracking is.

(You understand what I mean, ante-factum or pre-factum, whatever.)

In the absence of a budget, you classify your costs as they arise. You receive a tidy summary of expenses later. Although not immediately helpful, it is nonetheless useful.

When you create a budget, you classify your costs ahead of time:

• You allocate money to the categories you intend to use it for as soon as it appears in your bank account.

• When an expense transaction is entered, it is immediately subtracted from the associated category, updating the amount that remains.

This allows you to quickly see how much money remains in each category. You must move funds from another category if you have overspent.

Making a budget starts an instant feedback loop.

• If you overspend on takeout, your budget will suffer.

• Get made to replenish the takeaway category with money meant for utilities; • Get mentally kicked and make a promise not to do it again.

It will take some time for you to develop the habit of not spending money that you haven't budgeted for.

Budgeting has one additional significant advantage. You always know exactly where your money stands because your budget is updated in real real-times provides you peace of mind in addition to preventing unintentional expenditures. You can stop worrying about whether you'll have enough cash at the end of the month to pay your bills.

Ensuring there is actual revenue when it comes to your finances is the only thing left to worry about when you're budgeting.

It's also quite freeing.

A budget is essentially just a strategy for your finances, to put it simply. You can take charge of your finances and utilize your money wisely with the aid of a well-thought-out budget, ensuring that you have enough to cover your expenses, build savings, and continue to enjoy life now.

To gain a better understanding of your spending patterns, particularly areas where you tend to overspend, the first step is to categorize your monthly expenses into budget categories. You can begin allocating your expenditures

based on your unique financial situation once you've determined your fundamental budget categories.

Making a budget has several advantages. It can assist you in controlling your expenditure so that you can move closer to objectives like debt relief or home ownership. To prevent taking on excessive debt or putting yourself in a difficult financial situation, it can also help you determine how much you can afford to spend on items like rent, a mortgage, or auto payments. It is a good idea to create a budget so you know exactly where your money is going, even if you don't currently have any specific savings goals.

Indeed. A crucial step in learning how to save more money is making a budget. You can more effectively prioritize your spending by dissecting your costs and taking a close look at where your hard-earned money is being spent. It is simpler to evaluate your spending and make necessary cuts when you have a budget. It also aids in the planning of achieving financial objectives like setting up an emergency fund, clearing debt, purchasing a house or vehicle, or even financing a wedding or a trip of a lifetime.

All set to create your very own budget? Here's a detailed explanation of what to do.

The first thing you must do is determine your net income. Net income is the amount left over after taxes, benefits, and expenses are deducted for an individual or business.

In the world of business, net income is the amount that remains after all costs have been paid, such as taxes, salaries and wages, and the cost of commodities or raw materials. Net income is the amount of money that remains after taxes, health insurance, and retirement payments are deducted for an individual. A sign of good financial health should ideally be net income larger than expenses. The entire amount generated, or gross revenue, is subtracted from expenses like taxes and interest payments to arrive at net income. Let's say Jane gets paid every two weeks, grossing $3,350. Her total tax payments are $272.51 from the federal government, $46.61 from Medicare, $193.31 from Social Security, $102.48 from the state, and $125 from insurance. This leaves her with a net income of $67,862.34 a year, or $3,350 − $272.51 − $46.61 − $193.31 − $102.48 − $125 = $2,610.09 every week. Knowing net income is crucial since it makes it clear how much may be allocated to both discretionary and living costs.

Net income is significant since it is the amount that a person should consider when making purchases and creating a budget. After taxes and other payroll deductions, a person earning $4,000 per month from a new job might only have $3,000 (or less) left over. They would soon find themselves in a dire financial situation if they spend $4,000 a month. Instead, they could begin saving money for the future if they examine net income and ensure that scheduled spending is less than net income. The next step is to calculate your expenses after you have that figured out. To create the ideal budget that will meet your demands and desires, it is essential to comprehend the two different types of spending. Both fixed and variable expenses are incurred. Fixed expenses are those that always cost the same amount, such as rent or a mortgage. These are the expenses that you can budget for and are probably already included in your normal spending plan. Although these expenses might arise at any time, they usually take the form of monthly or annual payments. Your property/school taxes, tuition and/or childcare expenses, cell phone and internet services, student loan payments, rent or mortgage payments, car payments, insurance premiums (auto, home, renters, health, dental, life, etc.), subscriptions and memberships (meal kits, fitness memberships, etc.), and other expenses. Expenses classified as variable are those whose amount and frequency vary. These costs are more challenging to budget for since they might change based on several variables, including unanticipated expenditures and discretionary spending. Grocery, petrol, eating out, entertainment (concerts, movies, etc.), personal care (haircuts, massages, etc.), home, vehicle, and property upkeep, health care, hobbies, clothes, and utilities (gas, water, and electricity) are a few examples of frequent variable expenses. Since fixed expenses are usually due at predetermined periods, budgeting for them is generally simpler than for variable expenses. Because they are less predictable, variable expenses are more difficult to budget for in advance.

Apart from that, a big part of budgeting is learning to distinguish between requirements and wants. The easiest way to do this is to keep in mind that desires are items you enjoy but aren't essential to your everyday existence, whereas needs are the things you can't live without.

For instance, a lot of fixed expenses, like rent and insurance, are "needs." Conversely, some variable expenses, such as dining out and clothing purchases, can be classified as "wants." Of course, some variable costs—

like groceries, healthcare, and utilities—also have to be paid for.

The 50/30/20 budget rule states that you should set aside 50% of your money for "needs" and 30% for "wants." The remaining twenty percent goes toward investments and savings.

Prioritizing and setting aside money for necessities first is usually advised as many of them are fixed costs. This is where things get a little trickier with variable costs. Despite their unpredictability, variable expenses can still be budgeted for. Assessing your usual expenditure in these categories for a few months before creating your budget is the best method to accomplish this.

You can include the amount you spend on each variable item each month, on average, in your budget. You can reevaluate over time to be sure you're budgeting the right amount.

Examining your fixed and variable costs more closely will help you identify areas and strategies for cost savings if your goal is to cut back on expenditure.

Review your fixed expenses.

Saving money on fixed expenses is not impossible, but it can be challenging. You have a few options for reducing these expenses. For instance, you can look for a more affordable phone or internet plan and cancel any subscription services that you can live without or that you no longer need. An employee benefits program might provide you with access to lower insurance rates.

Reduce erratic expenses

There are some simple behavioral adjustments you may begin making in your day-to-day life to reduce your variable expenses. For instance, consider something for a bit before buying it. Consider if you are making this purchase out of need or want. If it's a desire, think about if it would be wiser to put it off if you haven't yet saved enough money.

You can start cutting back on your expenditure by first evaluating how crucial the variable cost is to your happiness and well-being.

Any budget must account for both fixed and variable costs to stay on track.

When creating your budget, you should first carefully examine your fixed and variable costs to identify areas where you may make savings. Although it is impossible to plan for everything, you may spot trends and use that information to reach your financial objectives.

Funds for Emergencies

Individuals who have had significant unplanned costs are likely to tell you one of two things: how glad they were to have an emergency fund or how challenging it was to locate the cash they urgently required. Like other financial matters, planning is essential to surviving the inevitable storms of life that we will all encounter. barely one in four Americans do not have any retirement savings, and the median emergency fund balance among workers is barely $5,000, according to the 21st Annual Transamerica Retirement Survey.

In essence, an emergency fund is money saved aside for unforeseen circumstances in life. In the unlikely event that you lose your job, the money will allow you to live comfortably for several months without incurring debt. Consider it as a kind of insurance. You're paying yourself money that you can spend later, as opposed to premiums

to a company. If a bad thing were to happen, it would be simple and quick to get the money.

The demand for an emergency fund grew as a result of the COVID-19 outbreak. According to a YouGov study done for Forbes in April 2021, about 40% of respondents who had emergency money were compelled to use it as a result of the pandemic, with 73.3% of them depleting half or more of the fund and 29% spending it entirely.

Many people lost their income and employment as the entire nation was placed under virtual lockdown. The costs of their daily lives persisted. Though it took some time and not everyone was eligible, the government did intervene to assist.

In what ways did the pandemic alter the previously mentioned pre-pandemic statistics? Six months into the epidemic, Bankrate conducted another survey and found that 35 percent of Americans reported having less emergency funds than they had six months prior, while only 13 percent reported having more. Just 16% of Americans indicated they felt "very comfortable" about their emergency savings overall.

According to the most recent Bankrate poll, which was published on July 21, 2021, 51% of Americans, including

25% of those without a fund at all, have less than three months' worth of spending in their emergency reserve.

Only 17% of people have more money in savings than they did before the pandemic, and 34% have less. Of those who had emergency savings, 48% were not "comfortable" with them.

It makes sense to monitor spending during the pandemic and account for it when estimating future needs. Most likely, this is not the final one. The Center for Global Development estimates that there will be a pandemic in the next ten to twenty-eight years and in the next twenty-five to fifty-seven years.

Even less serious incidents, like a broken limb or a wrecked car, can necessitate the need for emergency money.

So, what is the ideal amount of money to have in an emergency fund?

It is recommended by numerous institutions and financial experts that you maintain an emergency fund with a minimum of three months' earnings. In this manner, in the unlikely event that you lose your job, you'll have enough cash to last a few months until you locate another job.

However, the sum may differ based on your preferences and financial situation.

Determine your living expenses first. Add up the amount you pay each month for groceries, utilities, rent or a mortgage, and car expenses. A minimum of three months' worth of living expenditures should be covered by your savings, and ideally, up to six months.

Vanguard. "What's the Right Emergency Fund Amount?"

You might be able to depend on the support of a family member who has a steady income if you live in a double-income household and it is improbable that both income earners will be unemployed at the same time. You might be able to survive on the barest minimum if you have insurance coverage that will protect you against unforeseen emergencies. But everyone ought to make it a point to save at least a small amount for unforeseen costs.

Maintaining Your Objectives

Creating and adhering to a strategy is the most reliable approach to accomplish most objectives. Create an account that is only accessible online, such as an Esavings account.8 Schedule automatic transfers from your regular bank account to this new account by your paychecks, so that you won't even see the funds in your original account.

When you accumulate enough money in this liquid account, you can move some of it to high-yield savings accounts or short-term bonds, where you can still access it with ease when you need it.

There can be moments when it will be alluring to spend the cash on a big wedding, a trip, paying off debt, a down payment on a new house, or any other unforeseen large expense. For this reason, you ought to compile a list of allowable outlays for your fund at all times. Make sure these are real emergencies, like living expenses during unemployment, unexpected medical expenses, home repairs from a fire or natural disaster (or major furnace breakdown), unexpected veterinary bills, unplanned auto repairs, or unexpected tax bills.

The whole purpose of having an emergency fund is to keep you from having to borrow more money when you need it or from having to rush to get money at the last minute. Raising money to solve the situation is not what you want to be concentrating on.

Making Debt Payments vs. Savings

Debates abound on whether strategy should take precedence: preparing for emergencies or paying off debt. Each has advantages and disadvantages. Although paying interest on high-interest debt is a significant hardship, paying it off should always come first. That being said, you should still set aside money each month for other goals.

The wisest course of action is to strike a balance. This keeps you from needing to borrow money in the event of an emergency and helps you develop sound financial habits. When paying off debt, take into account the amount you can realistically add to your emergency fund at the same time. This is the first step toward developing sound financial habits, even if it is only $25. Your fund will keep growing as your debt load decreases, even if it does so slowly.

Living below your means can be difficult, but when that rainy day comes, you'll be glad you did, and it won't have a significant negative effect on your financial situation overall. Concentrate on altering your perspective. You are the only one you can truly rely on to pull you out of difficulty. Reliability should not be placed on friends, family, insurance, the government, or even good fortune. Everyone has bad experiences occasionally, thus achieving financial stability ought to be prioritized equally with taking care of your physical health. A savings account designated for use just in case of an emergency, such as unforeseen medical expenses, job loss, or need to pay for an unanticipated auto repair, is known as an emergency fund.

Should I Save for an Emergency Fund Before Paying Off Debt? This has advantages and disadvantages. Since paying off high-interest debt is such a financial pain, it usually should come first. Having said that, it's wise to reduce high-interest debt and develop the sound financial habit of contributing, even slightly, to an emergency fund.

An emergency fund is a vital part of any person's overall financial strategy. This would assist you in covering your costs in the event of an emergency or unanticipated circumstance. This amount from your total investments or savings will provide you with enough assurance to get through such situations. Even if Covid was highly extraordinary, the unusual times caught everyone off guard, and in those circumstances, savings and other financial resources were crucial. Similarly, such a fund might be quite helpful in the event of an unanticipated job loss, business losses in the case of a self-employed person, serious illness, etc.

A financial goal is a target or milestone that you want to reach in terms of your money. This can be debt repayment, stock market investing, vacation savings, or emergency fund savings. When my financial objectives are connected to my needs, wants, and deepest ambitions, I've had the most success. Even if a financial goal outlines your desired outcomes, reaching those goals still requires action on your part.

I want you to know that financial objectives change with time. Don't forget to account for changes in responsibilities and lifestyle when establishing financial goals.

2022 marked my sister's birth year. Life looks quite different now than it did five years ago, or even a year ago since she left my job to work for herself the previous year. Though many people adopt new financial goals for the year, think about checking in with them from time to time to see if they still make sense. You are free to decide otherwise. Your objectives will change. Just as nothing in life is set in stone, neither should your personal finance objectives.

Why is goal setting important, one may wonder? Financial objectives are comparable to ship or aircraft navigation. Even if the ship or plane manages to land at all, it will not do so without them.

These objectives are essentially financial plans for the future, estimating the amount of money needed for particular expenses like a dream home purchase, a child's marriage, or further schooling. It is necessary to project or predict future expenses in line with the rate of inflation. Following estimation, investments must be made in viable possibilities that can produce those returns. Assume someone requires approximately. The real setting enables us to envision and shape our future. For example, he needs to invest $10,000 each month for 20 years in an asset class that can increase at a rate of 12% pa to buy a house with $1 million after 20 years. It assists us in evaluating our current situation and establishing our goals.

Finding clarity can be greatly aided by beginning with your goals or desires in life. We can also be more decisive when we have goals. We have the freedom to choose our priorities, our future selves, and how we wish to present ourselves to the outside world. Setting goals is crucial because it helps us define and attain achievement while also keeping us on course.

Short-term, mid-term, and long-term financial goals are the three different categories of financial objectives.

Within a year, reach your short-term financial objectives.

Often, short-term objectives serve as benchmarks or stepping stones toward longer-term objectives. However, they are also independent.

Usually, short-term financial objectives center on debt repayment, savings, and budgeting.

Long-term financial objectives span more than three years, whilst mid-term financial goals are set for a period of one to three years.

Goals related to long-term finances include financial independence, asset accumulation, and retirement preparation.

You build an employment arrangement to supplement your income in this way. This is significant because it facilitates efficient financial planning and management. You can use it to set financial objectives and monitor your progress toward reaching them. A budget also enables you to spot potential areas of overspending and modify your spending patterns to be within your means. A budget can also assist you in setting aside money for essential costs like a down payment on a home or a child's education. All things considered, it's a useful method of making sure you can maximize your earnings and reach your financial objectives. Applications and platforms exist that could assist you in accomplishing this;

1. Mint:

One of the most widely used free budgeting applications is Mint. It provides a wide range of functions, such as budget planning, credit score monitoring, bill reminders, and spending tracking.

Users can link their credit cards, investment accounts, and bank accounts together with Mint to get a comprehensive picture of their financial situation. Additionally, the app provides tailored analysis and advice on how to cut costs and save money.

2. **Individual Resources**:

Offering both investment tracking and budgeting capabilities, Personal Capital is a potent budgeting app. It gives consumers a concise summary of their earnings, outlays, and net worth.

The program automatically classifies expenses and imports transactions through integrations with financial institutions. Users of Personal Capital can also monitor their retirement accounts, investment portfolios, and fees to better tailor their investing strategy.

3. You Need a Budget, or YNAB, is:

A well-known budgeting program called YNAB focuses on "giving every dollar a job." Users may use it to set aside money for different categories and make a budget depending on their income. With YNAB's real-time synchronization feature, customers can monitor their financial status on numerous devices and always be up to date.

In addition, the app encourages users to set up a proactive budget and save money by offering instructional materials.

4. Each Dollar:

The approachable budgeting tool Every Dollar was developed by personal finance guru Dave Ramsey. It lets users manage their income and expenses and make custom budgeting categories, all with an emphasis on simplicity.

The main advantage of Every Dollar is that it emphasizes the zero-based budgeting approach, in which each dollar is given a distinct function. While the paid edition of Every Dollar offers features like detailed reporting and account syncing, the free version is still a great place to start.

5. **Pocket Guard**:

Simple budgeting software like Pocket Guard provides a quick overview of a user's financial situation. It tracks income and spending, automatically imports and categorizes transactions, and offers spending pattern insights.

In addition, Pocket Guard enables users to make budgets, establish savings targets, and get notifications when they are about to exceed their spending limitations. The software is a favorite among users of budgeting apps because of its ease of use and straightforward UI.

It's advisable to have four budgets. quarterly, monthly, every two weeks, and every year. The rationale is that all of your year's expenses may be tracked and subtracted to account for payments made at various intervals.

If you had a weekly budget, for instance, it would be primarily allocated to expenses for transportation and meals. These are daily expenses, so they convert easily into weekly budgets and are simple to monitor. But it's easy to forget about things like monthly phone payments, quarterly electricity bills, annual car registration, etc.

In a similar vein, it can be challenging to determine your monthly food budget without first dividing it down into weekly costs.

Because of this, I find it easier to keep track of everything and determine how much money I should set aside each week to cover all incoming bills when I create an annual budget that includes all of my spending and then breaks them down into monthly, fortnightly, and weekly categories.

Maintaining a budget needs strategy and perseverance. If you're having trouble making ends meet, remember that two-thirds of Americans don't even have a budget! Some people may make a budget, but they struggle to deal with the obstacles that come with it. Nevertheless, you may overcome your budgetary difficulties and start down the path to financial success with perseverance and careful planning.

You can track your monthly expenses by creating a budget. Budgeting will help you avoid running out of money and improperly saving as well. Making a budget and following it keeps you from living paycheck to paycheck and guarantees that you don't overspend.

Setting up a budget enables you to save money, pay off debt, and increase your investment portfolio. Budgeting can also teach you how to live within your means, which will help you stop wasting money on unnecessary purchases.

Ten Budgeting Difficulties and Solutions

Take a look at these ten typical budget problems and the essential actions you may take to solve them.

Having financial indecision

Financial indecision is the worst kind of indecision there is. Being indecisive when it comes to money might stall you and keep you from reaching your objectives. Even though creating a budget might seem intimidating, starting is the most beneficial thing you can do.

It will take longer for you to take charge of your finances the longer you put it off. One of the main obstacles to budgeting is indecision, but you can overcome this obstacle if you have a little financial drive. There are two strategies to deal with indecisiveness about money.

Make your budget first.

No one starts their life running. We crawl, then walk, then we run. The same applies to overcoming indecisiveness. Making a budget should be your first priority. Don't dwell on what challenges budgeting will bring; just focus on starting. Once your budget is made, you may address each budgetary issue as it comes up, one at a time.

Automate your finances

You can arrange for your payments to be paid automatically each month by automating your accounts. By putting your money on auto-pilot, this step can help guarantee that your payments are paid on time and relieve some of your decision-making burden (to an extent).

Get financial help

Getting financial guidance is a great method to get past financial indecision! There are tons of free courses and resources to help you reach your financial goals.

Impulsive shopping

Impulsive purchasing is one of the most difficult budgetary obstacles to overcome. Most people have engaged in impulsive buying. In actuality, 156 impulsive purchases are made annually by Americans.

Approximately $450 is spent on impulse per month, which adds up to almost $5,000 annually!

Do you own a copy of the film Confessions of a Shopaholic? Can you imagine the excitement of getting a new shoe or pocketbook, only to be disappointed when you see your credit card bill? If so, you might have an addiction to buying, which would be terrible for your finances. Here are some strategies to break the habit of your impulsive purchases:

Determine what triggers you.

Impulsive buying is typically the result of a bigger problem. One way to avoid shopping impulsively is to identify the true cause of your problems instead of going shopping when you're upset.

The next time you find yourself tempted to shop, sit down and write down your thoughts and the events of that day. You might be shocked to learn that buying is merely a coping strategy and that seeking assistance is the first step towards becoming well.

Minimize your in-person and online shopping excursions.

Purchasing is similar to dieting. There is always a temptation, and there are instances when it is just simpler to restrict your exposure. Restrict the frequency of your shopping trips and steer clear of stores that you are aware are weak points for a while.

This also holds for purchasing online. Try your hardest not to "browse" the stores until you can control your impulse buying.

Give yourself a small sum of money.

Everyone has to treat yourself occasionally, but if you do, make sure it fits into your budget. Give yourself a certain amount of money each time you go shopping as an allowance. In this manner, you can still have fun without going over budget.

Not setting financial objectives

Setting up monetary objectives is essential to conquering the difficulties associated with budgeting. You risk forgetting why you made a budget in the first place if you don't have a clear objective in mind. Setting and meeting financial objectives might help you achieve financial success by keeping you within your means.

Financial objectives include, for example:

Putting money aside for a trip

accumulating an emergency reserve

financing a wedding

Accumulating funds for an initial payment on a residential property

Getting ready for retirement

Setting both short- and long-term financial objectives is crucial. You can make those lofty aspirations more manageable by breaking them down into smaller, more achievable ones by setting short-term targets. Make a note of all your financial objectives when you sit down.

Using the incorrect budgeting technique

There isn't a one-size-fits-all approach when it comes to budgeting techniques. You can be employing the incorrect budgeting technique, which is one of the reasons you are having trouble with your finances. The trick is to choose the budgeting tool or template that works best for you out of the various options available.

You should look into the following examples of budgeting methods:

Budgeting in reverse

Budgeting with zeros

Budgeting by percentage break-out

Budgeting using cash envelopes

70-20-10 spending plan

80/20 spending plan

Budget: 30-30-30-10

Budget: 60-30-10

Make sure the budget you choose is something you can easily keep to!

The dread of having debt

Although ignorance is bliss, the lack of a financial strategy can be disastrous for your finances. One of the most challenging financial issues to date may be the idea of sitting down and totaling up the whole amount of debt you have. But making a debt payoff plan with your budget is the only way to take back control of your financial destiny.

Ignoring your debt will not only exacerbate it but also harm your credit. Find out how you can pay off your debt in several methods and incorporate them into your new spending plan.

Overindulging in restaurant meals

Overeating is one of the most frequent budgetary problems. In America, the average annual cost of eating out is an astounding $3,000! That is a sizable sum of money that you may use to fund your emergency fund in case of inclement weather. While eating out might seem convenient, it quickly "eats" through your budget.

Assume you eat lunch out five days a week for ten dollars a day. You might save $2,600 just by bringing your lunch. Set the first objective of packing your lunch each day rather than going out to dine.

Making a food plan and prepping your meals is the simplest approach to avoid eating out too much. In this manner, your mouthwatering meals are ready to consume.

Not setting aside money for savings

You may not be properly budgeting even if you are paying your expenses on time. You aren't planning for your future, for instance, if you don't include savings in your budget.

Paying yourself first is among the most crucial things you should do when creating a budget. Including savings in your budget is the fastest approach to saving money. In this manner, it establishes a sound financial habit and keeps you from being tempted to spend it.

Set aside a predetermined amount for your savings account or a specific proportion of your pay to start. To make sure you do it regularly, you can even set up automatic payments to your savings. Take on one of these money-saving challenges to make conserving money enjoyable!

Not maintaining a regular budget

Like most things, the secret to a successful budget is consistency. Maintaining a regular budget helps you stay on track financially and stops you from overspending. Continue using a budget calendar to make sure you are staying under your spending limit and paying your payments on time.

Additionally, you should regularly update your budget to make sure everything is accurate. Make sure your budget is current, for example, if your expenses rise or if your income fluctuates. Put a regular evaluation of your money on your schedule by scheduling a budget review.

Accumulating debt on credit cards

Reaching for that enchanted plastic card each time you go shopping is far too simple. But if you don't pay off your entire balance each month, you end up overspending on those necessities. Due to the high interest rates associated with credit card debt, it can be extremely costly.

Instead of taking on more debt, increase your emergency fund and savings. You may save hundreds or even thousands of dollars by making upfront payments for purchases rather than putting them on your credit card.

If you can't help but charge your credit card, keep it locked up somewhere secure instead of carrying it around in your wallet.

Unexpected costs

Unexpected expenses are a part of life, and managing them within a budget may be quite difficult. You must so increase the amount in your emergency savings account to be ready for any unforeseen circumstances. Things that can derail you include auto repairs, medical bills, and job loss.

To cover unforeseen costs, the objective is to accumulate three to six months' worth of living expenditures. Work on saving your first $1,000 and go from there to avoid getting overwhelmed by a large sum.

You can overcome your obstacles with budgeting.

Overcoming the obstacles of budgeting can assist you in adhering to your spending plan and assisting you in effectively managing your finances. Recall that the key to your success is selecting the appropriate budgeting technique.

To stay motivated, don't forget to create a vision board or list of your financial objectives.

It's difficult to escape a financial rut once you've fallen into one.

When you do, you frequently find yourself going deeper and deeper.

How would you begin? On what do you concentrate? And how can you keep yourself from getting worse off?

Even while improving your financial status can be challenging, it is not impossible.

Numerous people have succeeded in doing so without having to create multibillion-dollar businesses or earn millions of dollars in stock market gains.

No, these are just regular individuals like us, with a lot of expenses to pay off, limited finances, and no stock market expertise.

These incredible success tales demonstrate that anyone can entirely climb out of a hole and fill it with earth to prevent falling into it again with a little effort and preparation.

Marina Ella Firsthand knowledge of Mint.com

Ella Marina was finding it difficult to keep track of her spending, particularly since each time she swiped her debit card, she had to recall a new set of digits.

It quickly became exceedingly difficult to keep track of every receipt and enter every purchase into Excel.

Fortunately, she came across Mint's budget setup. All you have to do is enter your basic financial data (bank account, loans, income, monthly bills, etc.), and the website takes care of the rest, estimating how much money you should have left over at the end of each month and providing useful guidance on how your spending stacks up against others.

Krissy was able to save thousands of dollars because of Mint's skillful management of her finances. She was able to streamline her spending such that almost all of her bills were paid in one paycheck, giving her several extra checks each month to support her in leading a life rather than just making ends meet.

How Carrie Rocha Used Your Money to Pay Off a $50,000 Debt in Less Than Three Years Carrie Rocha owed more than $50,000. She managed to pay off her entire debt in

2.5 years, despite losing her employment during that time.

Coupons are her covert weaponry. Not just any coupons, but carefully cut coupons, that is what she and her family did.

All too frequently, even when there is a coupon attached, people buy everything just because it has one. They then question why they aren't making any financial savings.

Instead, Rocha bought just essentials—especially ones that were already on sale—and soon discovered that she was rapidly saving a sizable sum of money.

The good news is that you may still save a lot of money online even if you no longer purchase newspapers (children, ask your parents if you don't understand what a "newspaper" is).

Simply select the ones that are most helpful to you, print them off, and start saving!

Geoffrey Lennon Learns How to Save Money the Middle Way

Geoff Lennon was struggling to save any money at all and balance his budget. He attempted to micromanage every dime but found it to be too complicated.

Then he attempted a laissez-faire strategy, which was more lazy-faire than anything else because he ceased recording any expenditures at all.

Not surprisingly, he lost it rather quickly.

Lennon eventually found a happy medium in the form of the Balanced Money Form.

Though it doesn't monitor every single item you do with your money, this middle-of-the-road strategy arranges your spending so that, ideally, less than half of it is allocated to "needs" (bills, food, gas, etc.).

The other half would be divided between savings for the future and anything you desire (games, toys, vacations, music, electronics, etc.).

Lennon was able to finally start saving money by following this strategy, and it might be able to assist you as well.

Despite having no financial knowledge, Doug Nordman retired early.

Doug Nordman, a former professional military man, decided he needed to spend more time fathering and less time working after having a child. Less income and more savings would result from this.

Thus, Nordman and his spouse were able to save in every manner possible, even though they freely acknowledged that they were not very financially astute and that they had made many mistakes along the road.

They avoided as much unnecessary expenditure as they could and embraced any free entertainment options, like the beach or library. They took on whatever maintenance or improvement project around the house that they could manage on their own.

After decades of saving and trying to find a portfolio that worked for him, Nordman ultimately took an early retirement in 2002 and hasn't looked back.

He chooses not to work, although he could take a job anyplace, so he spends his day having fun. He would much rather have fun, and he can do so now that he has figured out a workable financial solution.

These tales unequivocally demonstrate that you can save money, manage your spending, pay off debt, and even perhaps start retirement early.

All it takes is a little effort, intense concentration, and tremendous commitment.

Even while your narrative will ultimately be unique from the ones you just read, it's still possible that you could benefit from one or more of their tips.

Try it, and your bank account will thank you for the thousands of extra bucks you will have.

Chapter 3

Accept Your Actual Aspirations

What do your values mean to you, and how do they show themselves in your home, workplace, relationships, and financial situation? In the era of information overload and plenty, it is essential to establish a clear framework to support your values.

While it may seem simple, matching your financial status with your values may be a difficult task that frequently calls for outside assistance. To assist you in connecting your financial aspirations and ambitions with your values, we cordially encourage you to peruse the accompanying information.

Determine Your Genuine Principles

To begin, divide your values into two groups: the values you were raised with and the ones that bring you joy. The objective is to determine whether there is a distinction between the values you believe you have and the values that are meaningful in your life, even though there may be some overlap between the two.

For instance, you might have been instructed to put in a lot of effort and sacrifice yourself for a well-paying profession, but it might not be fulfilling you personally. If you work in a profession that pays less but whose good work and mission you believe in, you can feel greater fulfillment. Jim Taylor, a psychologist, suggests responding to the following three inquiries to begin this process:

What are the daily decisions you make in your life?

What pursuits truly make you happy to engage in and are you passionate about?

Which individuals and events make you feel particularly involved in and connected to the world around you? You can find the principles that genuinely fulfill you and make your life happier by delving into these questions. Constant unhappiness is a clue that you might not be living up to your genuine ideals if it has to do with your work, your money habits, or something else entirely.

Recognize Your Financial Attitude

It is also necessary for you to assess your financial thinking. Your life experiences have shaped your financial outlook. Your parents may have taught you wise financial practices. If you witnessed your parents' financial failure, you might have even picked up poor money practices. Your personal financial experiences, no matter what they may be, are crucial to understanding why you act the way you do when it comes to money.

It's critical to understand your financial attitude since it enables deliberate growth. The first step in altering a financial attitude is recognizing one that is poisonous or inadequate. You have more influence over how and when you make changes when you know what you want to alter.

Align your desired life with your actual life.

Your ideal life likely appears different from your reality after all this contemplation. You need to align your "living life" with the ideals that bring you happiness to achieve your dream lifestyle. Recall that these values serve as a bridge to the pursuits, encounters, and relationships that offer you the greatest sense of fulfillment.

So, what is the process here? It's been said that the calendar and the checkbook are reliable sources of information. Someone will understand what is essential to you if they see how you spend your time and money. Just take a moment to be honest with yourself: does your spending match your true priorities in terms of time and money?

If not, it's time to set monetary objectives that genuinely align with your principles. When your financial objectives align with your beliefs, money stops being the end goal and starts acting as a tool to help you achieve the genuine objective. You are now in a position where you can enjoy permanent bliss.

Is Happiness Something That Money Can Buy?

Money can buy happiness, as long as it is used in a way that is consistent with your principles, even if we all know that most material purchases can only bring temporary enjoyment. Arthur Brooks, a writer and Harvard "happiness professor," contends that although money cannot purchase happiness, it can, depending on the individual, improve well-being and life satisfaction. Here are a few instances:

Investing in Experiences: According to Brooks, spending money on memorable events, concerts, or travel usually results in a longer-lasting sense of enjoyment than purchasing tangible goods. These encounters produce priceless memories and boost feelings of contentment.

Supporting Others: assisting those in need, whether it be through charitable contributions or by lending a hand to friends and family. Acts of compassion and generosity can provide happiness and a sense of purpose.

Investing in Education: Increasing one's education or skill set can open up more job options, which can then translate into improved financial stability and personal contentment. This supports the notion that investing in one's development might pay off in the long run.

Reducing Financial Stress: Prudent money management and staying out of debt can help lower financial stress and anxiety, which improves general well-being.

Giving Back: Taking part in charitable endeavors and making contributions to causes that are dear to one's heart can offer a feeling of fulfillment and purpose.

The relationship between material prosperity and moral principles is a highly relevant topic in today's fast-paced world. Though it's frequently viewed as a tool, money can influence our choices and how we live. However, delving deeply into our underlying beliefs is necessary to grasp the real meaning of money for each of us. In this piece, we explore the complex relationship that exists between money and pursuing important things, looking at the fundamental motivations behind our goals. Fundamentally, money is a means for achieving stability and security. Being financially stable allows us to take care of necessities like food, shelter, and medical care. These essentials lay the groundwork for a happy existence, freeing us up to concentrate on our development and loftier goals. A value for responsible living and the desire to support ourselves and our loved ones without worrying about unforeseen setbacks are revealed by the quest for financial stability.

Additionally, money fosters personal development and progress. Our capacity to make educational investments, pick up new skills, and take on a variety of situations allows us to grow as people. Growth is valued because it represents a dedication to lifelong learning and an understanding that money may be used to broaden our perspectives and welcome change.

It is impossible to ignore the part money plays in fostering connections in the quest to understand its significance. Having money makes it easier to make enduring memories with loved ones, which strengthens bonds via common experiences. Relationships are valuable, which emphasizes how important it is to set aside funds for celebrations, travel, and quality time together—all of which add to a colorful life story.

The power of money transcends private spheres and offers chances to have a significant impact on society. Giving money to social causes and charity organizations shows that one is committed to their beliefs and wants to have a positive impact on the world. This tendency toward social effect is an indication of compassion, empathy, and a desire to make a lasting impression.

For a lot of people, having money is essential to following interests and pastimes that fulfill and offer happiness. The capacity to allocate resources towards pursuits that correspond with individual inclinations highlights the significance of expressing oneself and the need to preserve a fulfilling, balanced existence.

It becomes clear that each person's idea of wealth is closely entwined with their fundamental ideas and goals in the complex dance between money and personal values. Money's value is diverse, influenced by relationships, personal development, financial security, social effects, and pursuing passions. We can create a more balanced and purposeful approach to wealth—one that is in line with our true selves and empowers us to live meaningful lives—by acknowledging and accepting these underlying drives.

A person's fundamental values are a collection of ideas and precepts that guide their decision-making. These are the tenets that people live by and that direct their emotions, ideas, and behaviors. Early experiences, society, and parenting shape core values that are formed early in life. They assist people in defining who they are and what they stand for, as well as in determining what is important to them and ranking it. Consequently, a person's basic beliefs are essential to their development and well-being.

The Significance of Outlining Your Basic Principles

Establishing your core beliefs is essential because it gives you direction and clarity when making decisions, creating goals, and leading a happy life. The first step in ensuring that your activities are consistent with your ideas and principles is to recognize your core values, which are the things that are most important to you. When faced with complicated problems and tough choices, it's simple to get disoriented and confused without a strong foundation of principles. By defining your values, you may establish guidelines and expectations that will help you stay away from circumstances that contradict your beliefs and make choices that will advance your objectives. Furthermore, having a clear grasp of your values can help you develop a strong sense of purpose, meaningful relationships, and self-worth. It can also give you confidence in your activities.

Examples of fundamental principles for an individual

Integrity is among the most widely held essential values of a person. This concept entails telling the truth and being sincere in all facets of life, even when it's difficult. A man of integrity never wavers in his beliefs because of convenience or self-interest. Accountability is another shared value. This entails accepting accountability for your deeds and their results. In addition to being trustworthy, responsible individuals make an effort to address issues and accomplish goals. Another fundamental human value that is frequently mentioned is compassion. It is important to show others compassion, decency, and empathy. Those who are compassionate want to lessen suffering as much as they can since they have a strong connection and warmth for other people. Perseverance is, after all, a fundamental personal value. This value entails remaining committed to your objectives and on course in the face of difficulties and disappointments. Perseverance is valued by those who have a strong work ethic, are tenacious, and can overcome challenges to realize their goals.

How a person's basic beliefs affect their ability to make decisions

A person's guiding principles are crucial while making decisions. Our moral and ethical judgments are influenced by the ideals that we cherish. Our fundamental beliefs support and steer us in the right direction when we find ourselves in a difficult situation. It's critical to realize that making decisions involves more than just selecting an option; it also entails upholding your moral principles. You feel content and at ease when you make decisions that are consistent with your ideals. Bending your ideals, on the other hand, can cause you to experience regret, remorse, and dread. To overcome life's obstacles, we must ascertain our basic values and use them as a compass.

Determine your basic principles: a methodical approach

Taking stock of your life and your priorities is the first step towards discovering your basic values. Think about the ideals that were in place at the time and why a certain experience had an impact on you. Was the pursuit of justice and equity your driving force? Which did you value more, creativity or dependability? You can get an understanding of your motivations and priorities by looking at the values that have shaped your behavior in the past. Furthermore, thinking back on past errors and decisions can highlight moral principles that were previously disregarded but are crucial for both professional and personal growth. Since this step may expose painful truths about yourself that you were previously ignorant of, confidence and honesty are necessary. However, this is an essential stage in discovering your basic principles and setting up the framework for a happy existence.

connecting your basic principles with outside factors

Since these values are frequently strongly embedded in your ideas and behaviors, it can be challenging to strike a balance between them and outside pressures. It would be beneficial, though, if you were able to function in a more expansive social setting, where other influences might potentially contradict or undermine your central beliefs. You can become adept at this balancing act by regularly reviewing your views and principles and engaging in introspection.

You can discover the sources of outside influences and assess whether they support or contradict your ideals by engaging in this introspective process. You might also look for groups, associations, or people who have similar beliefs to your own. These networks can offer you the safety nets you need to maintain your moral principles when faced with opposition. In the end, striking a balance between your fundamental beliefs and outside influences necessitates an ongoing process of introspection, assessment, and action.

Share with others your fundamental beliefs.

It's crucial to have the ability to communicate your basic values since it will help you both personally and professionally. Not only does sharing your values make others more aware of who you are, but it also inspires them to follow in your footsteps. Making decisions is also made easier when you are aware of your basic values since you can use them as a reference to make sure your choices are consistent with your views. Establishing deeper relationships and fostering trust are further benefits of sharing principles. Furthermore, by aligning your conduct with shared values, articulating your principles can help foster a more happy and productive work culture. In general, developing better bonds with others and living a more satisfying life might result from sharing basic personal values.

Lead a life that is consistent with your main principles.

A life that is in line with your basic beliefs will make you very happy and fulfilled. You have a feeling of direction and purpose when your activities are in line with your values, which makes it simpler to navigate the decisions and problems of daily life. You take charge of your life and follow your inner compass, as opposed to being reactive. Because you are less affected by societal pressures and other people's opinions, you may become more resilient and self-assured as a result. Rather, you'll be able to lead a life that is authentic and in line with your beliefs. While it may require some reflection and difficult choices, living a life that is in line with your basic principles has enormous advantages that can improve many facets of your life.

These days, it's easy to get swept up in the frenzy of worldly desires and lose sight of what counts. Many people in this society of relentless striving and spending end up in a state of unfulfillment where their actual needs go unmet. Imagine living a life where we take the time to breathe, to be present, and to enjoy life's little pleasures rather than following the newest trends.

Imagine living a simpler life where the focus is on being in the now. It reminds me of seeing a youngster play, who is engrossed in the present and finds great joy in even the most basic things. This method questions the conventional wisdom that links success to financial gain. Do these standards serve our best interests, and if so, why do we adhere to them? It's time to consider and possibly revise our definition of success.

In all of its raw beauty, nature teaches us the value of connection and presence. Contemplate the way of life of the Puri tribe, which is intricately linked to the environment. They are the epitome of living in balance with, rather than opposition to, one's environment. Their existence, free from the complications of contemporary life, provides a glimpse into the deep serenity that results from a life of simplicity and connection to the natural world.

I discuss my personal experience through the craziness of living a life devoid of mindfulness while thinking back on mental health. It's an open admission of the difficulties encountered when a person loses contact with their inner self and chases after false dreams of happiness in worldly possessions. Despite its difficulties, this voyage shows the way to a happy and peaceful existence.

A significant metamorphosis occurs when one embraces simplicity. It brings clarity and tranquility, much like the first light of dawn after a long, night. Important insights can be gained from the Puri tribe's teachings, which stress the value of living in harmony with the natural world and the present moment. Finding out again what gives life purpose is more important than merely rejecting consumerism.

Thus, I implore you, my dear reader, to live in the now and find happiness in life's little pleasures. The sheer, unadulterated joy of simply existing is like reestablishing contact with an old buddy you've forgotten about for a long time. This is about achieving balance and realizing that true happiness frequently rests in the smallest of moments rather than in the grandeur of worldly accomplishment. It doesn't mean giving up on ambition or ambitions.

Recall that you are not the only one who feels overpowered by today's fast-paced culture. A lot of us are looking for a purpose in life other than financial gain. I implore you to appreciate the elegance in simplicity. Reconnect with the delight of being present, just like a child does with the little things in life. Together, let's question the status quo and ask why we pursue goals that frequently leave us feeling unfulfilled. Your happiness, serenity, and mental well-being are priceless. Together, let's redefine success as we go—not by what society considers successful, but by what truly makes us happy and fulfilled in life. Now is the perfect moment to begin living a happy and thoughtful life. Accept the here and now, learn to live simply, and observe as your life begins to weave itself into a lovely quilt of significant events.

Chapter 4

Financial Resilience

We discussed extensively in the last chapter how your values can influence your ability to make financial judgments, and how crucial it is that we consider these beliefs while making decisions. We'll talk about demonstrating adaptability in the dynamic world of finance in this chapter. There are many unknowns in life, therefore we must constantly be able to rise to the challenge with fortitude and skill. You're negotiating the dynamic world of money. You must develop the flexibility and abilities necessary to succeed in the face of unpredictability. This leads me to the concept of financial resilience. You must approach everything in life with realism, understanding that anything can go wrong and that it is our responsibility to get back up after falling.

The terms "resilience" and "resiliency" have become widely used since the September 11, 2001 incidents. The ability to function successfully and keep a positive view in the face of extremely stressful situations has been characterized as resilience in children, families, communities, and the country as a whole. Resilience is the capacity to persevere in the face of adversity and "roll with the punches."

The capacity to weather life events that affect one's assets and/or income is known as financial resilience. Individuals are impacted by certain financially difficult circumstances, such as divorce, unemployment, handicap, and health issues. Others have an overall impact on society, including terrorism, stock market declines, and recessions. Financial resources like savings, health insurance, and well-paying work help people become more resilient financially. Human capital, which economists define as all of the information, abilities, experiences, and other personal attributes that people have to "sell" to prospective employers, is another resource for financial resilience. Financial resiliency is also enhanced by social capital. This entails a network of relatives, friends, neighbors, coworkers, and other individuals who may offer both financial and emotional support in trying times. Enhancing one's financial resilience can also be achieved by implementing the suggested financial strategies outlined in Small Steps to Health and Wealth. Here are five instances:

• Preserve a modest ratio of debt to income. The monthly payment amount for consumer debt, such as credit card bills and auto loans, should not exceed fifteen percent of one's monthly income. For instance, dividing $275 in debt payments by $2,500 in net compensation results in an 11% consumer debt-to-income ratio (275 divided by 2,500).

• Keep a three-month emergency fund stocked with essentials. Maintain this cash in liquid assets like short-term CDs, money market mutual funds, or credit unions.

• Never think of your training for a career or education as complete. To enhance human capital and maintain employability in the cutthroat labor market of today, keep learning new, marketable skills.

• Invest in sufficient life insurance to shield dependents from the loss of a breadwinner's income and disability insurance to sustain income in the event of an illness or accident. Become more knowledgeable about financial matters so that you may make wise financial choices.

The year 2008 was terrible for people everywhere. The knowledge that we were all in this together was the only consoling idea. I recently saw the new Netflix documentary series "Madoff: The Monster of Wall Street," which brought back some unpleasant memories but also got me thinking about the important lessons that the terrible period had imparted to us. After we lost half of our savings, I wondered how we would ever be able to replace the lost money in time for our children to attend college. I'm only now feeling grateful for those challenging years. Realizing that no one will be as concerned about our money as we are was a wake-up call. It compelled us to look for alternatives to stocks as investment vehicles and prospects. Thankfully, we were able to bounce back, but it took some time. To reduce our risk, we had to reevaluate our investment strategy from the ground up. It's important to only invest money that you can afford to lose entirely because every investment carries some inherent risk. Financial setbacks are difficult to overcome, but not insurmountable.

Some may argue that it is useless. Any money I do manage to save is quickly spent on unanticipated expenses. Some people might claim that no matter how hard they try to stick to a budget, something always seems to throw it off. You're most certainly not alone if, after battling to stick to a budget, you've stated anything similar. However, if you took the time to review your bank records, credit card statements, and invoices, you could probably anticipate the great bulk of your spending. You can begin handling your finances as though you had a monthly bill for everything you owe, even though you won't necessarily receive one. Having a home or automobile requires upkeep and repairs. You will ultimately have to pay for a doctor's appointment or prescription if your health care plan has a deductible and copay. You'll probably also go to see relatives or friends or purchase gifts for them.

It goes without saying. Therefore, even if they may be surprising, you really couldn't call these charges unexpected. Even though none of these expenses are urgent, you should budget for them because you may reasonably anticipate them.

An excellent place to start is using the "square foot rule." This means that you should set aside money each year for normal home upkeep and repairs, which come to roughly $1 per square foot on average. You should be saving $1,500 a year, or $125 a month if your home is 1,500 square feet. Even if you won't have to pay it annually, you will in the end if you stay in your house long enough. To cover major housing bills, you should be saving at least that much. When a pricey repair is necessary, you'll then have the cash on hand. If you are aware that your furnace or roof is nearing its end, you may need to set aside even more money each month. Open a high-interest savings account and set aside money for house repairs. You can create 10 distinct "savings buckets" under your account with the online bank Ally to assist you in achieving particular savings objectives.

Your automobile may also be a barrier. Use Edmunds' Total Cost of Ownership Calculator to get an idea of how much you need to set aside for automotive maintenance to help you overcome this challenge. To find out how much maintenance and repairs will cost you over the next five years, input the make, model, and year your automobile was manufactured. For instance, Edmunds estimates that in 2020, owners of a 2015 Taurus Sedan should budget roughly $2,600 for maintenance and repairs. Be proactive and budget at least $200 every month if you anticipate spending $2,600 on your automobile annually. By doing this, you can keep yourself from charging auto repair expenses to a credit card that you might not be able to pay off at the end of the month. The figure at the bottom of your service invoice might not even come close to covering the cost of your repair bill, given that credit card APRs typically range from 15 to 22%. And keep in mind, even if you avoid having any auto issues this year, you'll still have a sizeable sum of money saved up for future repairs or the down payment on your new car.

Healthcare costs are a common source of financial strain. The primary causes of bankruptcies in the United States are medical bills and lost productivity due to sickness and injuries. Try to save up at least the amount of your health plan's deductible to reduce the likelihood that you will be caught off guard by this challenge. Aim to accumulate a $1,800 yearly deductible in 12 months by allocating $150 each month. Eventually, you want to gather the maximum amount of money that you have to pay out of pocket. If your meds are expensive, compare costs. You can't assume that the drugstore you often visit is offering the best deal available.

Prescription medicine costs can be reduced in several ways.

Holidays, festivals, birthdays, and get-togethers with relatives may all drain your finances. But now that you are aware of when they will occur, you must make plans for them. Determine in advance how much you will spend on forthcoming family and friend events to help you overcome this budgetary difficulty. Then, rather than waiting until the event is imminent, put money aside each month to pay for those costs. These kinds of costs are a necessary component of your budget since they are a part of your cost of living. They will undoubtedly make you fail if you leave them out. The secret to an effective budget is to try to forecast your future spending. By setting aside money ahead of time, you can maintain your spending plan and allocate more funds to emergency savings and retirement investments. Holidays, festivals, birthdays, and get-togethers with relatives may all drain your finances. But now that you are aware of when they will occur, you must make plans for them.

Determine in advance how much you will spend on forthcoming family and friend events to help you overcome this budgetary difficulty. Then, rather than waiting until the event is imminent, put money aside each month to pay for those costs.

These kinds of costs are a necessary component of your budget since they are a part of your cost of living. They will undoubtedly make you fail if you leave them out. The secret to an effective budget is to try to forecast your future spending. By setting aside money ahead of time, you can maintain your spending plan and allocate more funds to emergency savings and retirement investments.

Even if you're making big debt payments, you still need to start saving for emergencies. Include a line item for emergency savings in your budget so that you will have money on hand in case something unforeseen occurs. You will examine every expense closely as you create a budget. However, it's simple to revert to previous spending patterns over time and stop recording the amount you spend each time you use your credit card. Think about making use of internet resources like Mint or Tiller Money to make tracking your expenditure easier. If you think of yourself as a rookie when it comes to knowing money and how to accumulate wealth, you're not alone. You may obtain information to alter your financial future, though, as evidenced by the fact that you are here. Numerous emotions, including worry, pride, remorse, embarrassment, and more, can be triggered by money.

Furthermore, these money thoughts are typically holdovers from your early years.

If money is a scarce resource in your family, you may develop a scarcity mindset. If talking about money was frowned upon when you were a child, it might influence how you handle money in your partnership as well. Rewriting your financial story, embracing an abundant mindset, and making more financial decisions based on your beliefs can be necessary.

Unexpected costs are a major cause of debt accumulation and can throw a kink in anyone's plans. You understand how difficult it is to get ahead on your payments if you already have a lot of debt or if you owe money at extremely high interest rates. Making progress toward your financial objectives and debt repayment can be facilitated by using a budget, which is a great tool for tracking where your money is going. Remember that creating a good budget requires more than just setting it and forgetting. Particularly in the beginning, you'll need to keep an eye on your development and adjust your budget as necessary. or each time a big shift occurs in your life. But when you see your debt levels going down and your savings increasing, all of the work you put in to overcome the barriers and difficulties of good budgeting will have been worthwhile.

Achieving financial wellness involves more than just hoarding; it also involves planning. Every stage of life has its own special prospects and financial challenges. Every significant life milestone causes the financial environment to shift and change constantly. Many of us are still figuring out these unfamiliar waters, even if some of us have firsthand experience with the difficulties of purchasing a home or saving for retirement.

Chapter 5

Increasing your wealth

We covered what to expect when you decide to take control of your money in the last chapter, as well as how crucial it is to make financial decisions without letting outside influences sway you. We will now talk about developing your money and the best approach to achieving it in this chapter. Growing your money is crucial because it may help you reach your financial objectives and offer flexibility and stability. You may create a financial safety net to rely on in difficult circumstances, such as a recession or a loss of income, by growing your investments and savings. The ability to make decisions about your life, like being able to retire early or take time off to travel, can also come with having more money. Moreover, increasing your wealth might assist you in reaching particular financial objectives, such as property ownership, kid education costs, or accumulating a sizable retirement fund. All things considered, building wealth is an essential first step toward financial independence and stability.

Invest.

Investing is the best financial decision you will ever make. Investing can make your hard-earned money work for you, even though you may receive a consistent paycheck from your job. You can accumulate enormous wealth over time that you can utilize for retirement, your children's college education, or any other financial objective with the aid of a well-managed investment portfolio. Though it's generally accepted that investing is a wise decision, there's another crucial piece of information that has to be considered: what should you invest in? One of the main reasons that beginning to invest can be scary is that many people are unsure of what to invest in or where to begin. Thus, these are a few of the most popular methods for investing money.

Stock market investment is widely recognized as a highly favored method for increasing one's wealth. Purchasing business shares entitles you to dividend payments and the possibility of capital gains, which could result in a profit. Before making investment conduct research on the many stock kinds available, including income stocks, growth stocks, and blue-chip stocks.

During the past forty years, U.S. equities have outperformed bonds, savings accounts, precious metals, and most other investment categories in terms of returns. Over nearly every 10 years in the last century, stocks have beaten most investment classes and have historically yielded average annual returns of 9% to 10%. Returns such as these are comparable to the growth of $10,000 over 30 years when compounded at a rate of 10% to around $175,000. Why are American equities such excellent investments? because you own a business as a stockholder.

You legally own a portion of the company, for instance, if you possess shares of Alphabet's (GOOG -0.18%) (GOOGL -0.05%) Google, Apple (AAPL -0.96%), or Amazon (AMZN 0.89%) stock. And your firm increases in value as it expands and becomes more profitable along with the economy.

Investing in U.S. equities is, in the words of renowned investor Warren Buffett, "a bet on American business," and it has been a winning wager for more than 200 years. Additionally, certain companies pay dividends, which can

make them good choices for investors seeking to generate income from their portfolios.

Investing (either fully or partially) in mutual funds and/or exchange-traded funds (ETFs) is an alternative if you're concerned about investigating and choosing specific stocks. Investing in an S&P 500 index fund, for instance, will distribute your funds among the 500 companies that comprise the index. So, it wouldn't be disastrous if any one of them failed.

ETFs and mutual funds are comparable. They create a portfolio of stocks or other investments by pooling the money of investors. The primary distinction is that ETFs are traded on significant stock exchanges, allowing you to purchase shares at any time the market is open. Mutual funds are not nearly as liquid as stocks; they only price their shares once a day.

Increasing wealth is the most crucial stage in the long run. Bonds, which are essentially loans to a government or corporation, might help you maintain your current level of wealth once you've accrued some and are getting close to your desired level.

Three primary categories of bonds exist:

Corporate bonds are issued by businesses, and the yield on these bonds is determined by the creditworthiness of the issuing business. Known as "junk bonds," these bonds are the riskiest but also have the highest yields. Corporate bond interest is taxable in both the federal and local jurisdictions.

State and local governments issue municipal bonds; despite the name, this can also apply to debt issued by counties and states. Higher tax bracket investors find municipal bonds appealing because their income is exempt from most taxes.

The US government issues bills, bonds, and Treasury notes. National governments issue debt securities known as sovereign bonds or sovereign debt to cover their expenses. Usually rated with an extremely high credit rating and a low yield, these bonds are issued by extremely unlikely governments. Treasuries are the name given to federal government bonds issued in the United States, and gilts are the name given to bonds issued by the United Kingdom. Treasury securities are still liable for federal income tax, but they are not subject to state or municipal taxes.

The majority of large brokers allow you to purchase individual bonds, but for most investors, purchasing mutual funds and exchange-traded funds (ETFs) that invest in bonds on your behalf is the best option.

All a bond is, is a company-issued loan. The company receives the money from investors who purchase its bonds rather than going through a bank. The interest coupon, or the annual interest rate paid on a bond represented as a percentage of face value, is what the corporation pays in return for the capital. The business repays the principal on the loan's maturity date and pays the interest at predetermined intervals (often annually or semiannually).

Unlike stocks, bonds' terms—a legal document that describes the bond's features—can differ greatly from one another. Before investing, it's critical to comprehend the specific terms because every bond issue is unique. There are specifically six crucial characteristics to search for in a bond.

Bondholders can choose between two payment methods for their investment. The interest that bonds receive regularly before they may be redeemed for par value at maturity is known as coupon payments.

Certain bonds have unique structures. Bonds with zero coupons have no coupons; the sole payment due at maturity is the face-value redemption. Since zeros are typically sold for less than their face value, interest can be calculated on the difference between the purchase price and par value.

One kind of hybrid instrument that combines the characteristics of stocks and bonds is convertible bonds. These are standard fixed-income bonds with the option to convert into the issuing company's equity. If the issuing company's share price displays significant gains, this creates an additional profit possibility.

The bond market is essentially driven by the same risk/return considerations that drive the stock market, despite its seeming complexity. An investor might become a proficient bond investor after they grasp these few fundamental phrases and metrics that reveal the well-known market dynamics. The rest is simple once you get the hang of the jargon.

Action items to ensure financial stability both now and in retirement

A crucial first step toward achieving financial security is setting short--, mid-, and long-term financial goals. You'll probably spend more money than you should if you have no clear goals in mind. Then, when you want to retire or when you need money for unforeseen expenses, you won't have enough. You may find yourself in a never-ending cycle of credit card debt and worry that you'll never have enough money for adequate insurance, making you more susceptible than necessary to deal with some of the biggest hazards in life.

As the world discovered during the pandemic and as many families discover each month, even the most cautious person cannot be ready for every eventuality. Anticipating future events allows you to analyze potential outcomes and make the best possible preparations for them. This should be a continuous process so that you can adapt your goals and way of life to the inevitable changes that will occur.

ESSENTIAL NOTES

Goal-setting, encompassing short-, intermediate-, and long-term objectives, is the first step in prudent financial and retirement planning.

Establishing an emergency fund, cutting debt, and creating a budget are important short-term objectives.

Important insurance coverage should be among your medium-term aims, and retirement should be your main long-term objective.

You have the chance to formally examine your goals, make any necessary updates, and assess your progress from the previous year during your annual financial planning. Take this chance to create goals if you haven't done so before to put yourself—or yourself and your family—on solid financial ground. Financial experts suggest setting the following goals, which range from short-term to long-term, to help you learn how to live comfortably within your means, lessen financial difficulties, and save for retirement.

Short-Term Budgetary Objectives

Establishing short-term financial goals provides you with the groundwork and confidence boost required to accomplish longer-term, more ambitious goals. These first steps can be reasonably easy to achieve in as little as a year: Create a budget and stay with it. Build an emergency reserve. Reduce the outstanding balance on your credit card that is impeding your progress.

Establish a Budget

You can't know where you are going until you know where you are right now. That involves setting up a budget, you might be shocked at how much money is slipping through the cracks each month."

A convenient method to monitor your expenditures is by utilizing a complimentary budgeting software such as Mint. It will consolidate the data from all your accounts into a single location, enabling you to categorize each spend. An alternative approach to creating a budget is to browse through your bank records and previous months' bills, identifying each cost using a spreadsheet or by handwriting it down.

You can make better judgments about where you want your money to go in the future when you can see how you are spending it and use that information as guidance. Do you think eating out is worth the extra cash you spend each month, given its convenience and enjoyment?

Well, that's fantastic if you can afford it. If not, you've just learned a simple method for making monthly savings. You can search for methods to cut costs when dining out, substitute homemade meals for some takeaway or restaurant meals, or do both at once.

Create an Emergency Fund

You should set aside money in an emergency reserve especially for unforeseen costs. $500 to $1,000 is a decent starting aim. Once you reach that amount, you should increase it to a point where your emergency fund can handle more severe financial setbacks, including being unemployed. If you didn't have an emergency fund before the COVID-

19 pandemic, you likely wished you did. Furthermore, you might need to renew it if you have one and have already used it up.

To cover your fundamental necessities and financial commitments, I advise saving at least three months' worth of expenses, but ideally six months' worth—especially if you work in a location with few job opportunities or are married and employed by the same company as your spouse. According to her, you may fund your emergency reserves by making at least one budget cut.

Putting things in order and arranging them is another method to accumulate emergency funds.

Having a yard sale or selling unwanted stuff on Craigslist or eBay can earn you additional cash. Think about making a passion your part-time job so you can use the money for savings.

Create a savings account and use your budget to decide how much you can save each month to open the account and set up an automated transfer until you reach your emergency fund target. Save any bonuses, tax returns, or even an extra monthly paycheck as soon as it appears in your checking account. If you are paid bimonthly, this occurs twice a year. The likelihood is that the money will be spent rather than saved if you wait until the end of the month to transfer it.

Even though you undoubtedly have other savings objectives, including retirement savings, setting up an emergency fund need to be your first priority. Your savings account is what establishes the financial stability required to accomplish your other objectives.

Clear Your Credit Card Debt

On whether to start building an emergency fund or paying off credit card debt first, experts can't agree. Some people advise starting an emergency fund even if you don't currently have any credit card debt because any unforeseen costs will push you farther into debt if you don't have one. Some advice paying off credit card debt first because the interest is so expensive and makes reaching other financial objectives much more challenging. Select the philosophy that most resonates with you, or combine elements of both at once.

My recommended approach to paying off credit card debt is to make a list of all your obligations ranked from lowest to highest interest rate, then pay the minimum amount due on everything but the highest-rate bill. Make extra payments on your card with the highest interest rate using whatever extra money you have.

The debt avalanche is the name given to this technique. The debt snowball strategy is an additional one to think about. Regardless of the interest rate, you pay off your debts using the snowball method from smallest to greatest. The theory is that when you pay off the smallest loan, you'll feel a sense of accomplishment that will motivate you to pay off the next-smallest bill, and so on, until you are debt-free.

For people who can't afford the statutory minimum payments and have unsecured debt (credit card debt, for example) totaling $10,000 or more, debt negotiation or settlement may be an alternative. These businesses, which are overseen by the Federal Trade Commission, help customers reduce their debt by up to 50% in exchange for a fee that is usually a percentage of the total debt or the amount of the reduction. The customer should only pay the fee following a successful negotiation.

This method can help consumers pay off debt in two to four years, according to Gallegos. The disadvantages are that debt settlement might lower your credit score and that clients who fail to pay their bills may face legal action from creditors.

Mid-Term Budgetary Objectives

It is now time to start working toward your midterm financial goals after you have established an emergency fund, paid off your credit card debt, or at least made significant progress toward those three short-term objectives. These objectives will build a link between your immediate and long-term financial objectives.

Obtain Disability Income Insurance and Life Insurance.

Do you support your spouse or kids with your income? If so, you should get life insurance to cover them in the event that you die too soon. Term life insurance is the most affordable and least complicated kind of life insurance, and it can cover the needs of most people.

You can get the best deal on a coverage with the assistance of an insurance broker. Most term life insurance companies undertake medical underwriting, and you can undoubtedly find at least one company that will sell you a coverage unless you are very sick.

It is advisable that you obtain disability insurance to safeguard your earnings while your employment. According to him, "most employers provide this coverage." "If they don't, people can get it on their own until they're retirement age." Should you sustain a serious illness or injury that prevents you from working, disability insurance will replace a portion of your income. If you lose your ability to produce an income, it can provide a bigger benefit than Social Security disability income, enabling you and your family, if any, to live more comfortably than you otherwise would. Another reason having an emergency fund is crucial is that there will be a waiting period between when you become unable to work and when your insurance benefits begin to pay out.

Repay your student loans.

Numerous people's monthly budgets are severely impacted by student loans. Reducing or eliminating those payments will free up funds, which can facilitate your retirement savings and other goals. Refinancing into a new loan with a reduced interest rate is one tactic that can assist you in paying off your student loans. However, exercise caution: Refinancing your federal student loans through a private lender may result in the loss of some of its advantages, including income-based payments, deferment, and forbearance—all of which can be helpful in difficult circumstances.

Think About Your Dreams

Midterm objectives can also involve purchasing a first house or, eventually, a vacation property. Perhaps you currently own a house and want to start saving for a bigger one, or perhaps you want to enhance it with some substantial renovations. Other midterm goals include saving for college or the fees associated with starting a family.

When you've set one or more of these goals, start figuring out how much you need to save to make a dent in reaching them. The first step to realizing your desired future is to visualize it.

Long-Term Financial Goals

For most people, accumulating enough money for retirement is their top long-term financial objective. The common rule of thumb is that you should save 10% to 15% of every paycheck in a tax-advantaged retirement account like a 401(k) or 40 (b) if you possess the option of opening a Roth or conventional IRA. But to make sure you're saving enough; you need to figure out how much you'll need to retire.

Determine How Much You'll Need for Retirement

Here are suggestions on performing a fast back-of-the-envelope calculation to gauge your readiness for retirement:

Calculate how much you want to spend each year on living throughout retirement. Your first budget, which you made when you set out to achieve your short-term financial objectives, will help you determine how much you require. Your retirement healthcare expenses may increase.

Deduct the amount of money you will be paid. Incorporate pensions, retirement programs, and Social Security. You will then have the necessary quantity that your investment portfolio needs to cover.

Calculate the amount of retirement assets you will require at the time you wish to retire. Based on your annual savings and present possessions, make this decision. You can conduct the calculations with an online retirement calculator. You are on schedule to retire if, at the time of retirement, 4% or less of this balance pays the remaining expenses that your combined Social Security and pensions do not cover 4.5%

The 15% savings rate and 45% income replacement rate serve as the foundation for the sustainable withdrawal rate for retirement in the United States.

You wouldn't run out of money in any 30-year retirement if, for instance, you started with a $1 million portfolio and withdrew $40,000 in year one (4% of $1 million), then increased the withdrawal by the rate of inflation each succeeding year ($40,000 plus 2% in year two, or $40,800; $40,800 plus 2% in year three, or $41,616, and so on). This is why 4% is frequently mentioned as a general guideline when talking about retirement.

In the best of circumstances, you would have run out of money in year 30, but in the worst case, you wind up with more money at the end of 30 years with 4%, he continues. The only warning that has to be given is that just because 4% of things have survived every situation in history, it does not mean that they will do so in the future.

To determine if you're on schedule to retire, here is an example:

A couple, 56 years old, hopes to retire in ten years.

Ideal yearly living costs $65,000

Social Security of Spouse No. 1 at age 66 $24,000 $2,000 a month

Social Security benefit of Spouse No. 2 at age 66 $24,000 $2,000 a month

Remaining requirements (to be funded by investments) $17,000

Total investments required, based on a 4% withdrawal rate

($17,000/.04), to cover remaining needs $425,000

Current balances in both spouses combined 401(k) and IRAs $250,000

Over the next ten years, further funds will be required. * 175,000 dollars ($17,500 annually, or roughly $1,460 every month)

*The rate of return that the existing investments would generate over the next ten years has been left out for simplicity's sake.

Boost Your Retirement Funds

The employer will typically match a portion of your income if you have an employer-sponsored retirement plan. They could contribute 3% or even 7% of your income. The most crucial action you can take to finance your retirement is to contribute enough to receive your full employer match, which will allow you to receive a 100% return on your investment.

The fact that people choose not to contribute to their retirement plans because they either "can't afford to" or "are afraid of the stock market" bothers me greatly. They overlook what I call a "no-brainer" return.

To give the money more time to develop and provide yourself a greater amount to retire with, financial advisor in Warrenville, Illinois, suggests making IRA contributions at the beginning of the year rather than the end, when most people choose to do it.

What Kind of Financial Objectives Are There?

A person might set himself a variety of financial objectives. Paying off debt, setting up an emergency fund, saving for a down payment on a house, preparing for a child's college education, feeling comfortable and financially secure, and being able to assist a friend or relative are a few of the more popular ones.

How Do You Begin Establishing Your Budgetary Objectives?

Using so-called SMART goals is one technique to develop financial goals. S is for specific, M for measurable,

A for achievable, R for relevant, and T for time-based in the acronym. Prioritize your goals by writing them down and then consider each SMART element. Establish a target retirement age as well as a quantifiable quantity of money you hope to have saved up for that time. Verify that the objective is doable and reasonable. Make it pertinent, and make sure you have a strategy in place to reach that objective within a given amount of time.

Likely, you won't make smooth, straight progress toward any of your objectives, but consistency is what matters most. Don't be hard on yourself if you have to take money out of your emergency fund because you were unexpectedly faced with a medical expense or auto repair one month and are unable to contribute to it; that's why the fund exists. Simply get back on course as quickly as you can. This also holds in the event of a job loss or illness. You may find that you are unable to save for retirement or pay off debt during that challenging time, so you will need to come up with a new strategy to get through it. Once you emerge from the other side, you may continue with your original plan, or perhaps a modified one.

The benefit of annual financial planning is this: Throughout the ups and downs of life, you can revisit, revise, and track your progress toward your goals. During the process, you will discover that your financial objectives can be met by the little things you do every day and every month as well as the larger things you perform annually and over several decades.

You record your revenue when you first create your budget. After that, deduct your costs, beginning with the necessities (sometimes known as the Four Walls). Your priority is the Four Walls, therefore before you do anything else, make sure your budget can pay for these (in this order):

Food Services Transportation Shelter

Make a list of everything else you need to pay for and rank it according to importance after taking care of things. Instead of realizing at the end of the month that you are short on cash for basic needs, you can ensure that your family is fed, your lights are on, you have a roof over your head, and you have enough gas in your car to drive to work by starting with the Four Walls.

After creating a budget, find areas where you can reduce your spending, or even better, eliminate it.

Are all those streaming services necessary? I understand if you feel attacked. However, consider what you could accomplish with the money you spare. $50 over here, $25 over there. This cutting/spending stuff could result in extra hundreds each month or thousands annually! When you believe you have exhausted all options, I am here to inform you that there are still a ton of methods to stretch your budget and increase your margin.

Here's a significant one: Give up eating out. (Yes, you will be my direct target.) But, since you'll know what's for supper at home, meal planning will help you resist the urge to get takeout. Knowing exactly what you need to buy each week will also help you save money on food and clear out space in your fridge and budget.

I understand that giving up anything feels bad, particularly if you're not used to saying no to yourself. Nonetheless, there will be a short-term cost for a long-term benefit. We are pursuing huge goals and developing sound financial habits so that in the future you can indulge in all of your favorite activities (such as dining out and traveling)! And during this trip, I think you'll come to realize that you can genuinely be content with less.

You are held back by debt. You have to pay for the Christmas gifts from the previous year in June. After that, you're left with the debt from your

December beach getaway. That isn't how you get ahead!

To be honest, debt is becoming more and more elusive. Plans such as "buy now, pay later" are becoming more common. At checkout, they entice you with the promise that you may pay for the air fryer in four simple installments.

Even on meal delivery apps, I've seen the "buy now, pay later" option! (All right, I'm becoming very upset now.) Fact: You cannot afford to split your meal order into four $13 installments. I'll go one step further, though: you cannot afford it if you are required to make any payments at all. Clearly.

One of the main things that keeps you in the paycheck-to-paycheck cycle is having debt of any type, as the payments deplete your hard-earned money. But now is the moment to end the pattern!

Here's how to do it: First, refrain from incurring any further debt. Avoid getting a new auto loan. Cut up those credit cards. Open a shop card and refuse to save 10% on that cardigan (believe me, it will end up costing you more in the long run).

Next, use the debt snowball to pay off any existing debt. It's the quickest way to finish those payments (trust and believe that debt was a doozie; I know this since I paid off all of my debt using this strategy).

Just consider this: What percentage of your monthly income is used to pay off debt? When your debt is paid off, you can have that much extra money in your budget! Payroll, goodbye. Hi there, advancement.

Raise your salary.

You most likely need to raise your income if you've created a budget and reduced your spending but are still barely scraping by. Can you put in more hours or work more shifts? Can you take on more clients as a freelancer? Should you look at finding another, higher-paying career entirely? Perhaps you should start a secondary business. Working as a barista, driving for Uber or Lyft, waiting tables, or answering phone calls are all excellent ways to supplement your income. If you can use your interests and talents to help others, that's even better.

While paying off debt, my favorite side gigs were baking wedding cakes, building websites, puppy sitting, teaching piano, cleaning houses, and babysitting. Setting your price is the best thing about side gigs. Who knows? Your side project might develop into your primary endeavor. Either way, the goal is to increase the amount of money coming into your spending plan.

You can then ease off on your spending a little bit after clearing your debt and building up your savings—or you may choose to keep working hard to achieve your other savings objectives, such as a house, college funds for your children, or retirement.

Don't raise your income to maintain an unaffordable lifestyle. If you're not careful, a pay increase may lead you to raise your living standards (a phenomenon known as "lifestyle creep"). All of a sudden, your bank account is overflowing with money, and you begin to spend more than you have ever done.

Your wealth is determined by how you use your income. Recall your initial motivation for wanting to raise your income. Remain focused, stronger, full, and adhere to your spending plan!

If you have just lost a significant amount of money on a major purchase, nothing makes you impatiently count down the minutes until payday.

Therefore, utilize a sinking fund to save money and make a cash payment if you sense an impending expense (such as noticing that the tread on your tires is becoming very worn). In this manner, rather than going over your entire monthly budget, you're saving a little each month.

Additionally, if you're living paycheck to paycheck, you should reconsider purchasing any large, unnecessary purchases—at least while you're working to pay off debt and build up an emergency fund.

Therefore, put off the trips and other items you desire but do not need, such as the fantastic gaming system your friend is selling or the new living room couch. Even if it's a fantastic price, you should hold out until your financial situation has improved. Though you may want to give up on some days. But keep your why in mind when things get difficult. The stronger the reason, the stronger the attempt, as I often remark. Consider your long-term objectives, such as purchasing that beachfront condo, giving your kids a better life, or traveling during retirement, if that helps. My spouse and I were aware that we needed to end the debt cycle to establish a stress-free family free from financial worries for both ourselves and our children. We needed money to make things easier.

Perhaps, though, you could focus more on the here and now and picture a life free from worries about overdraft fees or having your card denied. If so, pay attention to that. Whatever it is that inspires you to move forward. When you're putting in that extra grocery delivery shift, keep your why front of mind. When you find yourself wanting those shoes but not needing them, remember your reason for not clicking Add to Cart. When you make your coffee instead of using a barista, never forget why you did it.

It's difficult to make significant adjustments in your life and finances. However, you are more resilient. Allow your desired future state to motivate you to keep moving forward. I promise it's worth it.

You may feel like a rat on a wheel if you're living paycheck to paycheck. You keep traveling in circles and never seem to get anywhere.

Chapter 6

Creating a Couple's Budget

This chapter makes it very evident that couples are not excluded from leading the lives they choose and from achieving financial freedom in an attempt to impact the lives of everyone. Transparency is essential when it comes to financial matters involving your spouse. This indicates that you two are honest with one another regarding your financial situation, including your investments and any debts you may have.

Discuss the things you would like to get done together. Together, start saving for those objectives. Your family should always come first when making financial plans. It's not acceptable to lie to your lover about your money. It undermines confidence. You don't have to manage the other person's money if you plan together. Keep your money in check and be upfront with your partner while doing so. Establish shared objectives and collaborate individually, if you understand what I mean. Together with your spouse, create a budget. This is one of the less talked about aspects of marriage... A big part of learning to be married, or improving at it, is figuring it out.

There are other ways to define marriage, including equal partnership, merging, and union. Whatever you say about yours, you probably agree that the secret to happiness is communication. Discussing all significant matters, such as parenthood, sex, lifestyle decisions, and money, with your partner is essential. In actuality, one of the main causes of marriage failure is financial concerns.

ESSENTIAL NOTES

One of the main causes of marriage failure is a lack of communication regarding finances.

Together, you may create a budget that will serve as a framework to prevent financial arguments.

Utilizing financial tracking software can boost productivity and simplify the process of managing expenses.

A weekly "money date" can help you stay in touch, reach your financial objectives, and realize your life's ambitions.

The Solution Based on Budget

It's not always necessary for money to be a tense topic. The secret to managing money, regardless of your marital status—"soon-to-be," "newlywed," or "been in the trenches awhile"—is to create a financial plan or budget. Budgets don't have to be as complicated and challenging as they may seem. A budget is just an estimate of how much money you and your partner will make over a given period and how you want to spend it.

Together, begin by outlining a basic budget plan. After you and your partner have established a budget, all you need to do to stick to it is communicate with each other frequently. Ideally, you will track your continuous financial progress in a quick, accurate, and easy manner by using free or low-cost software (see more on this in Step 6). The seven steps are as follows.

Step 1: Make S.M.A.R.T. goals.

To ensure that your financial goals are geared toward both the present and the future, divide them into three categories: short-, medium-, and long-term. Your entire budget will be greatly impacted by your short-, medium-, and long-term financial goals. Short-term objectives, which include things like setting up a three-to-six-month emergency fund, paying off credit card debt, and preparing for a memorable trip, usually take one or two years to accomplish. The repayment of school loan debt, saving for a down payment on a home, and purchasing a new car with cash are examples of medium-term objectives. This may require ten years.

Saving for retirement is the most significant long-term objective that anyone may have. To achieve this, you must invest and save over the majority of your working life, which can last up to 40 years or longer.

An acronym that's frequently used in goal-setting is S.M.A.R.T. Although the terminology varies, the following are frequently used when creating financial goals:

Define your objective precisely in a few well-chosen terms. "We aspire to be owners of condos in the Bahamas."

Measurable: How will you know when your objective has been met? "What is the estimated cost?"

Achievable: It needs to be something you can afford to do, given your current situation. "Given our present financial situation and anticipated earnings in the future, can we save the amount necessary?"

Realistic: Does it make sense given your circumstances, even if it is achievable? "Is it alright if we choose to give up what?"

Temporal-based You may determine if this is a short-, medium-, or long-term aim by looking at your timeline. "How much time will this take?"

Test your goals using S.M.A.R.T. and make any necessary adjustments. If purchasing a condo in the Bahamas is too expensive or takes too long, consider purchasing a timeshare instead. or choosing a beach resort along the state line instead.

Some goals may need to be put on hold and reviewed at a later time, perhaps following a significant promotion or pay increase.

Step 2: Calculate Your Net Profit

After you've established your financial objectives, evaluate your monthly earnings. Your entire income prior to taxes and other deductions is known as your gross income. That isn't useful when making a budget, but make sure to include any money that is deducted for Social Security, retirement, or pensions because they will be needed in the future. Use your net monthly income, or take-home pay, when making a budget. This is the sum that you get before you start spending.

Your net income is probably steady if you and your spouse get a salary or an hourly wage. You will need to review the income area at least once a month if either of you earns sporadic income from commissions from sales, self-employment, or seasonal jobs.

Step 3: Total Required Outlays

Compulsory charges are those that you have to pay each month. Examples include housing, which can be paid for with rent or a mortgage; automobile payments; petrol; parking; utilities; payments for school loans or other loans; insurance; credit card payments; and food. Food may become "what's left over after all the bills are paid" for some individuals, but you and your partner should determine the absolute least amount you must spend on groceries and make it a required expense. Deduct the required costs from your take-home pay. For example, if your required expenses come to $4,000 and your combined monthly net income is $8,000, you have $4,000 to carry over to Step 4.

Step 4: Determine How Much You Must Save

To find out how much you need to save to meet your financial objectives (Step 1) and how much is covered by tax deductions for a 401(k), IRA, or pension (Step 2), consult Steps 1 and 2. Step 4 should include all of this before continuing. From the amount left over in Step 3, deduct the amount you must save (for retirement and other purposes). That is the sum allotted for the subsequent category, which is discretionary spending.

Assume that you have a total of $1,600 that you need to save every month. You will have $2,400 for the following step after deducting it from the $4,000 that was left over in Step 3.

Divide Up Discretionary Spending in Step Five.

Discretionary spending is precisely what it sounds like money spent on something you desire but do not require. Buckle up—you and your partner will probably have the most fascinating "discussions" around discretionary expenditure. Discretionary spending refers to the costs associated with the activities and pastimes you share, such as dining out, taking trips, watching cable or streaming media, or dressing alike for the ugly Christmas sweater party this year. It also takes into account your spending. This might be separate outings with friends, sports (e.g., golf for one, tennis for the other), or any of a variety of other things that you both engage in together or separately. Beyond the essentials, it may also involve your wardrobe, gadgets, and level of luxury vehicle ownership.

Make a list of every possible discretionary expense and classify it as "individual" or "joint" spending. Discretionary spending usually has its micro-budget, which is made each month using the discretionary money that is available. In the aforementioned case, you have $2,400 available for non-essential spending. It is unlikely to be the case every month, therefore you and your spouse will have to discuss discretionary spending regularly. You will frequently need to make sacrifices for this together. Conflict can be reduced if you are both willing to endure the same level of suffering. And although there may be some negotiating involved, getting married does often improve your financial situation.

Step 6: Choose the Software for Your Budget

The exciting part is about to begin. Equipped with your foundational budget, you will search for budgeting software that fulfills your requirements and that both of you find pleasant to use. Although practically any tool or software for budgeting will function, some include features tailored expressly for couples to utilize. Here is a description of three.

A budget is necessary (YNAB)

Zero-based budgeting, or "giving every dollar a job," is the foundation of You Need A Budget, or YNAB for short.1. The approach functions best for those who are prepared to take an active role in their finances and break old patterns.

Alexa may be used to access YNAB on Mac and Windows systems. It is a real cross-platform solution, with apps accessible for both Android and iPhone. The program does not track investments; instead, it links to bank and credit card accounts. Multiple users can share YNAB budgets, and the YNAB website guides how to budget together as a couple. The website includes weekly podcasts, videos, and training for those new to budgeting. After the initial 34-day free trial, YNAB is available for $11.99 a month (or $84 for the full year).

Honey Due is a budgeting tool made especially for couples. You and your partner can choose how much information to share using this function. This makes it possible to keep track of both individual and joint spending. Although there is an app for iPhone and Android, there isn't a web or computer version, thus all of the work needs to be done on a smartphone.

Together, you and your spouse can respond to transactions, talk within the app, set monthly limits for each area of spending, and inquire about dubious spending (from a shared account). The software is supported by over 10,000 US institutions, and best of all, Honey Due is free.3. Well-funded

The well-known envelope budgeting method is used by Good Budget, formerly known as EEBA. It asks you to split your monthly income into virtual "envelopes" for each category of spending. An envelope's value indicates when it is closed for the remainder of the month. Like YNAB, this program is cross-platform due to its web version, which can be browsed on any computer and syncs all budgets between devices.

Transactions from several accounts are automatically added to Good Budget in the premium edition. In the free version, all data needs to be manually entered. The simple envelope concept is reinforced with graphs and spending reports, and the setup is made simple by Good Budget's Getting Started instruction.

You can establish up to 20 categories or envelopes with one bank account on two devices while using the free version of Good budget. Email support is included in the paid edition, which costs $7 per month or $60 annually and permits an unlimited number of bank accounts and envelopes on up to five devices.4

Step 7: Arrange a Weekly Cash Meeting

Maintaining open and continuous communication is the last stage after choosing and launching the software. Set aside time each week for a "money date" to review and assess your objectives. Regular financial conversations will help you and your partner stay motivated to reach your objectives and be on the same page. It doesn't have to take five hours, especially because most of the work will be done by your budgeting program. A fun method to spend time together and manage your finances is to talk about your budget over a glass of wine or while preparing dinner.

The Final Word

Money conflicts can be avoided and your pair can achieve their goals by creating a budget, sticking to it, and checking in with each other once a week to assess your progress. What better way to strengthen a long-standing connection or get a new marriage off to the finest possible start?

Chapter 7

Crushing Debt in Every Situation

Financial difficulty can result from having excessive debt in several ways. It could be tough for you to make ends meet or your credit can worsen, which would make it harder for you to be approved for further loans like mortgages or vehicle loans.

Regarding debt, there are three facts:

Entering it can be enjoyable.

Leaving it behind is not.

The work is worthwhile.

This is because having debt is similar to living under a cloud. Reducing debt has the power to change lives. Why not follow in the millions of individuals who have already done so?

However, be aware that it entails more than just credit card repayment. It entails altering your spending patterns, developing a budget, keeping tabs on your spending, setting debt priorities, setting aside money for emergencies and retirement, and being aware of where to obtain support.

It's a meticulous procedure, and errors are common throughout execution. Here are a few of the more notable ones that you should stay away from.

First mistake: You don't alter your spending patterns.

Is your wallet or pocketbook running on autopilot? Do you spend your mornings at Starbucks? Purchasing groceries without making a list? Have a strong desire to purchase the newest iPhone model? Take a trip to Applebee's for dinner on your way home from work.

Your life is made more pleasant, practical, and stylish by such routines. Additionally, they permit unnecessary money leaks from your bank account.

Fix: Disengage the autopilot. Just think of the money you could save by changing your habits.

Look for less expensive options. A daily cost of $4.95 for a Caffe Mocha? If you consistently stop on the way to work, that works out to $99 every month. Before visiting the grocery store, make a shopping list and follow it.

Without the newest iPhone and three or four streaming providers, see how you fare.

Eat in more frequently.

The instances of over-expenditure are only signs. Consider the thoughts that went through your mind when you made those purchases to identify the issue.

Most likely, the response is "nothing." You were operating automatically. Switch that off, monitor your spending, and activate savings.

Error 2: Pursuing debt relief on your own.

It is possible, but it is also more doable. You just need a little assistance, but seeking assistance suggests you may have an issue. Some people might prefer their friends and family to remain anonymous.

Remedy: Obtain private, cost-free assistance. Nonprofit credit counseling organizations that employ licensed and skilled counselors provide it.

If you need serious medication for your financial ailments, they can recommend debt-relief options including credit consolidation, debt settlement, debt management programs, or even bankruptcy. In addition to helping, you create a budget; counselors can teach you how to avoid debt in the long run. Making the third mistake of enrolling in an unauthorized debt relief program.

Programs for debt reduction can help you escape your financial bind. Just keep in mind that digging takes labor. A program is undoubtedly scummy if it looks too good to be true.

Remedy: Don't trust in miracles for debt relief. Scammers targeting debt relief will charge exorbitant fees and make implausible promises. So, how can one select a reputable debt relief company? Check them out with the state attorney's office in your area, the Better Business Bureau, or the Consumer Financial Protection Bureau. Credit unions, universities, and military associations should be able to provide you with recommendations.

Remember that there's no magic bullet. Be patient; debt-relief programs usually take three to five years. Be prepared to extricate yourself as well. If an organization claims you won't have to, that's a bunch of bullshit.

Error 4: Not making a workable budget.

Eliminating debt is akin to going to war, if I may exaggerate. You will most likely wind up raising the white flag if you try to wing it.

Remedy: Draft a practical strategy for the fight. It will cover basic needs like food, housing, health care, insurance, and education.

Additionally, it will free up space for you to settle your loan.

The best place to start would be to cancel your credit cards. We'll now take a break to allow Visa addicts to complete their seizures. If you have to pay cash for items like eating out, movies, leather boots, and technological gadgets, you'll second-guess yourself.

Error 5: Attempting to settle several bills concurrently.

You have monthly bills to pay, such as utilities, auto loans, and mortgages. Then there are bills, such as credit cards, that you can pay part of. Many attempt to deal with each of these things every month. Poor decision.

Solution: Pay off the costliest one first. The bill with the highest interest rate is that one. Paying $100 toward an 18% interest debt is more logical mathematically than paying $50 toward the same debt and $50 toward a loan with a 6% interest rate. Pay off the debt with the higher interest rate first, then move on to the lower one.

Closing accounts after they are paid off is mistake number six.

Two cravings strike when you've finally paid off a credit card. You want to celebrate and permanently bury that sucker by closing the account.

Adhere to the first impulse. The latter will impede your ability to recover financially.

Solution: Keep the account open. It may seem paradoxical, but it's preferable to keep credit cards that aren't being used. Long-term credit account holders who use a tiny percentage of their credit limit are rewarded by credit scoring models.

Keep the card unless there's an absurd yearly fee. Simply said, don't use it.

Error 7: Taking out a loan from or stopping payments to a 401(k).

Many people have retirement savings that they could utilize as a lump sum to pay off debt. That's one approach, but you need to consider the big picture and ask yourself, "Do I want to die of old age wearing a McDonald's uniform?"

Remedy: Pay off your current debts without using your retirement money or a 401(k) loan. First off, taking early withdrawals usually carries heavy financial penalties. Secondly, a lot of employers match your retirement contributions, at least in part. That is a gratuitous payment.

Third, acknowledge the appreciation of retirement income. The more time it has to grow, the earlier you start contributing. Try to save five to ten percent of your income for retirement. Okay, if it isn't feasible. Don't raid your retirement, though. Working at the Golden Arches is not what your golden years are supposed to be about.

Error 8: Not putting money aside for emergencies.

A Bankrate analysis from January 2022 found that almost 56% of Americans lacked $1,000 in savings for an emergency. Are you prepared to hire a lawyer if something goes wrong with your automobile, your roof leaks, or your dog attacks a neighbor?

Solution: Arrange ahead. An emergency fund should cover three to six months' worth of costs. Include that in your budget even if it can take some time. Set aside 5% of your money for unforeseen issues that arise in life. You'll most likely get much better sleep if nothing else.

Error 9: Failure to confirm the accuracy of your credit report.

A 2021 Consumer Reports investigation indicated that approximately 34% of Americans discovered at least one inaccuracy on their credit reports. Should you choose not to file a credit dispute, you can be held accountable for the error of another person.

Check your credit reports as a remedy. You are entitled to one free credit report each year from each of the three major credit reporting bureaus: Equifax, Experian, and TransUnion. Check for inaccurate balances and/or delinquencies, as they might lower your credit score and make it more difficult to obtain a loan.

Error 10: Failure to prioritize paying off debt.

The typical American cannot simply keep accruing debt as though it will never fall back on them, unlike the federal government. If you ignore your financial hole, it will simply become bigger because of interest rates.

Solution: Pay attention to the issue and its resolution. Taking a credit card-sized piece of paper and listing the five bills you wish to pay off is one technique to help you focus. Put tape on your credit card. You'll be reminded each time you reach for that card that you're adding to the issue rather than solving it.

The easiest fixes are to create a plan, acquire a budget, and follow it. If assistance is needed, millions of Americans have found relief by using debt management programs to combine multiple monthly payments for their obligations.

Error 11: Failing to move your balance to more advantageous credit cards.

The use of credit cards is not always bad. When used correctly, they may be really useful. Let's say you have a $4,000 credit card debt with an interest rate of 15.99. You would save $600 in interest if you switched that to a credit card with a 0% interest rate for 18 months and paid $225 a month.

The solution is to apply for a credit card that offers 0% or an extremely low introductory interest rate for balance transfers, then move your existing credit card debt to the new card.

These cards, if you qualify, can give you the breathing room you need to take drastic measures with your credit card debt. Recall that this is an "introductory" pricing. It will increase dramatically after it expires. You can find yourself in worse shape than when you started if you don't pay it off in the allocated amount of time.

The Greatest Debt Relief Method

You can now avoid mistakes. What comes next?

The following are some actions to take to pay off debt. While some of them are redundant, they are nevertheless worth hammering home.

Examine your spending plan. Is there somewhere you can cut costs and free up some money to go toward your debt? One fewer evening spent dining out (saving at least $20). Every day, bring your lunch to work to save at least $20. At least $20 should be saved to watch the movie or athletic event at home. Ignore Happy Hour to save $20.

Your credit card was the source of your trouble, so bury it. For genuine emergencies, carry one in your wallet. Make cash payments for everything else. Giving out $100 cash is far more difficult than giving out a credit card. Making all of your payments with cash almost eliminates impulsive purchases.

Make a list before you go shopping. If all you have is a credit card, a grocery store or mall may be a dangerous place. List all of your desires. Purchase only the items on the list. Enter, then exit. Additionally, never shop for groceries when you're hungry. When one is starving, even spam appears appealing.

Split the bill: If your roommates are truly thrifty, they'll probably save even more money than that. You cut back on your expenses for housing, groceries, utilities, television, rent, and even transportation. Usually, the money you save from splitting expenses will be sufficient to significantly lower your debt on its own.

Look around the house one more time. Do you need cable TV that costs $100 a month? Is it reasonable to spend $50–$75 for a game of golf? Are you able to clean the house and mow the yard by yourself? What if you worked out without a gym membership? Having all those goods is nice, but only if you don't have any debt. Until the last of your credit cards are paid off, discard them.

Seek assistance - If debt is still causing you anxiety, go online to a nonprofit credit counseling organization and schedule a free credit counseling session. They assist you in organizing your issues, creating a budget that works for you, and determining which debt relief plan is ideal for you. The counselors possess certification and training. The best part is that it's free!

How to Reduce Debt More Quickly

Although it may not be enjoyable, you can quicken your financial recovery by tightening your belt. You should be able to treat yourself to an occasional golf outing or night out after taking these actions.

Make more money: The Bureau of Labor Statistics reports that in January 2022, there were about 5 million more job opportunities than there were workers available. Taking on a second job, even for a few hours a week, can be difficult, but the time invested will be worthwhile.

Pay all of your bills on time. When you miss a monthly bill payment, you're essentially giving money away. Banks, landlords, and credit card firms all profit handsomely from late fees. They can earn more money without having to put in any additional effort. Don't part with your cash.

Is anyone up for a garage sale? Most people own outdated laptops, TVs, workout gear, furniture, and clothing that they rarely use. Allow someone to remove your trash for a fee.

Unbudgeted income: You can receive money from an estate or a tax refund that you weren't prepared for. Put a weekend getaway out of your mind. Use the funds to pay off debt.

Request a rate reduction: Check your statement to see if you haven't looked at the interest rates you're paying, particularly on credit cards. Your card issuer will wish to keep you as a customer if you have been a reliable and punctual payer. Inform them that they can if they reduce your interest rate to the absolute minimum. In this instance, the adage "Ask and ye shall receive" ought to be applicable.

Request a raise: Companies have been making a lot of money lately, but the new tax laws should increase their profits even more. There has never been a lower unemployment rate. Because of these factors, there might never be a better moment to receive a raise. The worst thing that may occur is to hear "No" again. It may seem difficult to pay off debt when you are broke, but you may move closer to financial freedom by putting these strategies into practice. Remain dedicated, modify your spending patterns, and get expert assistance when necessary. By being tenacious and persistent, you may pay off your debt and secure a better financial future.

Chapter 8

Educating Your Children about Budgeting

Children who learn budgeting skills early in life have a higher chance of becoming financially successful adults. Learning how to create a budget is crucial since it will keep you from going into debt and enable you to save for future objectives.

In this chapter, we'll go over how to educate kids on how to make a budget and stick to it so they may achieve their objectives and manage their money well into the future.

A person's early financial education can be largely derived from the lessons learned at home. Recent studies reveal that parents are the primary source of the financial information and values that children carry into their adolescence and adulthood.

Furthermore, by the time they are 5 or 6 years old, youngsters are developmentally capable of saving, per a study published in the Journal of Consumer Affairs. However, it is best if they begin learning the fundamentals of ideas like budgeting and saving as soon as possible.

Teaching children the fundamentals of money management and budgeting will help them deal with the financial realities of adulthood.

Kids can understand budgeting as making a plan to help individuals utilize their money as efficiently as possible. Omar Ruiz, a marriage and family therapist with over ten years of expertise in counseling, recommends introducing and demonstrating the value of budgeting to young children through food. Food is an excellent example because it's a product they utilize daily and it costs money to purchase.

In an email to The Balance, Ruiz said, "You can explain that budgeting allows you to know how much food you can purchase." "Show that budgeting can help you use the extra money toward something else you need or want if you already have a certain type of food at home."

Kari Lorz, a qualified financial education instructor, sent an email to The Balance suggesting that you consider utilizing the bucket system to help your child feel at ease with the concept of budgeting. This technique assigns the youngster three mugs or mason jars: one for saving, one for spending, and one for gifting.

They can put their money into one of these buckets when they get paid, either by the tooth fairy or through an allowance system. As their money grows, "they'll be able to see that money is for three distinct things," according to Lorz.

Overspending is one of the most frequent reasons adults have financial difficulties.

Remember that every child (and family) is unique, with unique financial circumstances. Therefore, teaching strategies that are effective for one family might not be the greatest for another.

Describe needs vs. wants.

Assist your child in learning the distinction between needs and wants so they can learn to prioritize their financial spending.

"It's imperative that your child understands that needs come first and wants come second," stated Courtney Hale, the creator of Super Money Kids. "They should focus on meeting their basic needs with their finances before pursuing their desires in light of this."

Think about contrasting toys as wishes and clothes as necessities. You may clarify to your youngster that clothing keeps them warm and shields them from the elements. They desire toys for play even though they don't need them to survive.

Describe the Budget's Development in Detail

The first step in creating a budget with your child is to spend time explaining money.

You can demonstrate to younger children how income works by using your income or a hypothetical example, as most children do not have a regular source of income. You can take them through your entire list of expenses and demonstrate to them how you deduct required costs from your income to determine how much is left over for savings and other spending.

Depending on their age, they might receive money from the Tooth Fairy, their stipend, a part-time job, or gifts from family members. Fake money is another way to demonstrate income.

Assist them in totaling their earnings for a specific time frame, such as a week or a month. Subtract their expenses from their income by having your child write down and calculate all of their expenses (needs and wants included) for that period. Congratulate your youngster and let them know they have enough money to meet their needs and wants if the number is positive. If the answer is negative, let them know that they will either need to reduce their spending or earn more money to reach their objectives.

Creating and Modifying Budget Objectives

Help your youngster choose an expense-related objective, such as visiting an amusement park or purchasing a new video game. After that, assist them in making a chart to record the money your child makes.

Let them physically deposit the money they earn into a piggy bank or whatever every time they make any. Seek your child's assistance in updating the chart to monitor the amount of money in the piggy bank. Together, come up with a strategy for how much they must make every day or every week to reach their objective.

Tell your child that as they get older, their goals and income will change. They will need to stay aware of their varying needs, desires, and priorities. For instance, youngsters can misplace their piggy bank or receive extra cash for their birthday from relatives.

A good objective should consider the child's age and have a reasonable deadline. This should be completed in less than a month for a pupil in elementary school.

Make an effort to match the child's passions with the financial objectives you use in your budgeting education. If a child has a passion for art, for instance, saving $20 for a 100-piece art kit in two weeks might be an appropriate aim. Even while it requires time, energy, and ingenuity to teach kids about budgeting, the effort is unquestionably beneficial. Your child will be able to develop other sound financial habits and steer clear of typical problems like debt and overspending if they know how to make and follow a budget. This may position them for future success.

Julia would go to their grandparent's place for the large family lunch once a month with her cousins. Every year, they eagerly anticipated the day when their grandfather would hand them some cash "so you can buy yourself something." After that, every child would dash to buy wine gums, sweets, or chewing gum. The parents, grandparents, aunts, and uncles said that with their behavior, the kids would never learn how to handle money. Thus, they suggested a unique examination wherein the kids would have to demonstrate, throughout the course of a year, exactly what they could manage to obtain with those meager coins.

While some of the youngsters considered saving their money, the two youngest ones, Ruben and Nico, paid no care and kept using it all on candy. They would often laugh and tease their cousins while flaunting their goodies in front of the other kids. Clara and Joe were so incensed about them that they were unable to endure saving their money any longer. They went along with Ruben and Nico to buy candies with what little they had as quickly as possible.

Due to his cunning, Monty began managing his money by trading it for goods and services or placing bets on other kids in card games. He soon caught the entire family off guard. He had made a lot of money with little work on his part. If he continued in this direction, he would become nearly wealthy. But Monty was careless, and he began to engage in increasingly dangerous transactions. After losing a wager on a horse race, he was left with nothing at all a few months later.

Alex, though, was a person of iron determination. In an attempt to win the competition, he saved and saved every penny he was given. By the end of the year, he had accumulated more money than everyone else. Better yet, he was able to purchase candies at a discounted price thanks to his large fortune, and on the day of the competition, he was given enough candies to last him for over a year. He still had enough money left over for a toy even after that. He emerged victorious, and his fellow cousins picked up valuable life lessons from him, including the value of saving and patience.

And there was Julia. Despite having a fantastic secret plan, poor Julia wasted her money and did not give her plan enough time to work, so she didn't enjoy the day of the competition. But she was so confident in the success of her plan that she decided to move forward with it, perhaps even changing the looks on her relatives' faces, who had appeared to be saying, "What a disaster that girl is." She was unable to preserve anything."

Just before the second year of her plan came to an end, Julia showed up at her grandparent's house with a violin and a large sum of money, shocking everyone. Hearing her play was even more stunning. She performed it quite well.

Though the family was unable to pay for Julia's violin tuition, everyone knew that she was incredibly passionate about the instrument. After meeting a homeless violinist in the park, Julia handed him all the money her grandfather had given her in exchange for teaching her how to play. The violinist consented, even though it wasn't much money, after observing Julia's excitement, and he joyfully taught her for months. After a year or so, Julia's curiosity and desire grew to the point where the violinist lent her a violin so the two of them could perform in the park. Their success allowed her to eventually purchase her violin and have some extra cash.

She received support from the entire family after that and rose to fame as a violinist.

And she would always remind folks how your greatest aspirations could come true with only a few well-spent dollars.

It's never too late to instill in your child (or grandchild) the value of "saving early and often," regardless of their age. Telling your child these true tales could be the motivation they need to start a lifelong saving habit that will only lead to greater and better things.

Chapter 9

When You Feel Like Quitting

Although it's simple to believe that money is an infinite resource, every dollar matters. Even though missing just seven dollars might not seem like much at first, the long-term effects of that sum can quickly stack up. Furthermore, losing out on those seven dollars could result in passing up a chance or making unfavorable financial decisions that could have been avoided. Understanding that financial difficulties are typical and learning how to make every dollar matter are crucial for this reason. The fact that financial difficulties are exceedingly prevalent is one of the most crucial things to comprehend. There is no shame in acknowledging when finances are tight and realizing that your circumstances are not exceptional, regardless of whether you were just laid off or are living paycheck to paycheck. Looking for tools to help you navigate through difficult circumstances, such as debt payback plans and budgeting software, can be quite helpful.

Although creating a budget can be difficult at first, it can be a very useful tool for handling financial stress. All sources of income should be included in a decent budget, together with the costs of necessities like rent or a mortgage, utilities, food, transportation, etc., to give a realistic idea of how much may be allocated to other things like clothes and entertainment. Setting aside some cash every month for savings is also beneficial since it keeps unforeseen expenses from totally ruining your finances. Last but not least, setting aside money for unforeseen emergencies in an emergency fund will assist make sure that, should the need arise, financial gaps are not too severe.

Being able to handle your money in trying times requires perseverance and commitment, but the benefits of having a solid plan for the future much outweigh the costs. Establishing wise financial habits early on can help one take charge of their finances, prevent needless debt, and provide peace of mind knowing that every dollar goes toward accomplishing long-term objectives rather than resulting in losses or debt from careless financial decisions made now.

It's normal for many of us to feel stressed about money in these uncertain times. The current state of the economy has made it harder for us to manage our finances, make prudent investments, and keep things stable in both our personal and professional lives. Prioritizing our physical and mental health is essential while navigating these financial challenges, though.

Acknowledge that experiencing financial stress is normal, particularly in these difficult circumstances. Recognize that many individuals are experiencing identical issues all over the world, thus it's acceptable to feel overwhelmed. It might be relieving to normalize the experience and reduce the pressure of feeling alone or strange in your challenges.

Knowing where we stand financially is essential to managing our money. We can make every dollar work toward our long-term objectives by assessing our financial situation and creating a practical plan of action. To make realistic plans and budgets, it is critical to have a comprehensive understanding of one's assets, income streams, and expenses. Future investing success also

depends on keeping up with changes in the investment industry, such as new asset classes or platforms that could help achieve certain objectives.

When going through difficult times, having access to trustworthy resources like debt repayment plans and budgeting tools can also be very helpful. These services frequently offer individualized advice tailored specifically towards individual needs, which helps ensure money is managed wisely rather than haphazardly throwing funds at any potential opportunity without fully understanding what's involved behind it. Additionally, having an emergency fund set up specifically for unforeseen events may lessen the stress brought on by unanticipated deficits while still leaving space for other monthly payments and necessities like groceries.

Lastly, any sensible investing strategy should always include a conversation with an experienced financial advisor. They can offer advice on the optimal way to allocate funds as well as recommend various portfolio options based on your level of risk tolerance, ensuring that you don't end up taking unwarranted risks with your hard-earned money. Making every dollar work toward reaching life objectives now will lead to greater security later on when one takes charge of their finances and uses wise methods.

Conclusion

To sum up, creating a personal budget and keeping tabs on all outlays and spending are essential components of personal money management. A specific sum should be placed in a savings account; according to some advice, you should always have three months' worth of living expenses set aside for emergencies. Finally, every school should need a course on personal finance education for the younger students. It is imperative for parents to take the initiative to educate their kids about banking, credit cards, interest rates, and credit. It was eye-opening to learn how important it was to see my actual expenditures on my budget sheet. But I now know where to minimize costs, and by making small changes to a few things and eliminating others, I will   notice a significant increase in money that I can put into savings.

www.ingramcontent.com/pod-product-compliance
Lightning Source LLC
Chambersburg PA
CBHW060036260726
48658CB00004B/1072